fika

The Art of the
Swedish Coffee Break

WITH RECIPES FOR PASTRIES, BREADS, AND OTHER TREATS

fika

Anna Brones & Johanna Kindvall

TEN SPEED PRESS
California | New York

contents

– – – – – – – – – –

what is fika?

Why is it that Swedish coffee is just *kaffe*, but coffee plus something to eat is *fika*? In Sweden the tradition of fika (pronounced "fee-ka") is as common as breakfast; something almost everyone does at least once a day. It factors into travel planning, work schedules, and even a relaxed weekend at home. Life without fika is unthinkable.

Functioning as both a verb and a noun, the concept of fika is simple. It is the moment that you take a break, often with a cup of coffee, but alternatively with tea, and find a baked good to pair with it. You can do it alone, you can do it with friends. You can do it at home, in a park, or at work. But the essential thing is that you do it, that you make time to take a break: that's what fika is all about.

At its core, fika means "to drink coffee." But the meaning goes much deeper. Fika represents an entire culture; it carries as much meaning for Swedish social engagements as it does for food customs. Fika is as indicative of a love of coffee as it is of a belief in maintaining tradition.

It's uncertain exactly when the fika tradition started, but the use of the word was noted as early as 1913. Using a form of slang, the two syllables of the Swedish word for coffee—kaffe—were reversed, resulting in a word pronounced "fäka," eventually evolving into today's commonly used "fika."

To have a real fika means using the classic recipes that everyone knows (what the Swedes call *klassiker*), either those from one of the Swedish cooking bibles like *Sju Sorters Kakor* (*Seven Kinds of Cookies*) or *Vår Kokbok* (*Our Cookbook*) or those passed down from one generation to the next. These classics are the baked goods so synonymous with fika that you can barely talk about coffee without getting an urge for one of them: cinnamon buns, the apple-rich *fyriskaka*, or even an open-face sandwich. They are the base recipes; the kind of culinary creations that many Swedes know by heart.

Eating is often emotional. It invokes a sentiment; we eat to celebrate, we eat to mourn. Separating food from how we feel about it is essentially impossible. Fika is the same; there's a personal and emotional connection to it, no matter which recipe you choose. A cup of coffee and a piece of chocolaty *kladdkaka*, for example, feels comforting. It is, in its own way, grounding. Baking it in turn is a reassuring act, making you feel safe, sound, and taken care of—a staple in which you know exactly what you're getting.

Whether they're consumed at a café or baked at home, each recipe in this book creates its own ambience, a feeling or an emotion, that is attached to the food itself. Kladdkaka is what you throw together when you're pulling an all-nighter in college, or when you have a friend coming over to discuss their latest love interest, or even cry about the last one. Semlor you only have in late winter and early spring, when the streets are still dark and cold and the warm lights of a good café are inviting.

Biskvier you get at a nicer, more traditional café, or bake up for a special affair. It invokes something fancier, something worth celebrating.

That's why fika is special; it fits into so many moments and seasons. You select what you eat for fika depending on what atmosphere you're trying to create: one dish is perfect to celebrate a birthday, another might be better simply to have with afternoon coffee by yourself. After all, fika is just as good a reason for catching up with an old friend as it is for hosting a Christmas party. Fika can be done anytime, anywhere, and with anyone.

Although it may be well meaning, "Do you want to meet up and grab coffee?" in English just doesn't carry the same weight as the corresponding Swedish question, *"Ska vi fika?"* "Should we fika?" is shorter, simpler; and every Swede knows exactly what it means: "Let's take a break, spend some time together, slow down." In fact, it doesn't even have to insinuate coffee; fika is all-inclusive and can be done just as well with a pot of tea or a pitcher of fruit cordial. Fika isn't just for having an afternoon pick-me-up; it's for appreciating slow living.

Therefore, it's not just because you bake a certain cake and serve a cup of coffee that you have fika. To truly fika requires a commitment to making time for a break in your day, the creation of a magical moment in the midst of the routine and the mundane. Fika is the time when everything else is put on hold. This book is intended to inspire you to do just that.

the importance of homemade fika

We both have Swedish backgrounds and thus have had the concept of fika ingrained in us from the beginning. As is typical in Swedish culture, both of our mothers regularly had something in the oven, be it a cake to

SWEDISH WORDS INSPIRED BY FIKA

fik — a place to have fika

fikapaus — taking a break to have fika

fikarast — a specific time in the day for having fika, like in a workplace

fikastund — the moment you have fika

fikarum — a break room, often with a kitchen, that is intended to be used for fika

fikaställe — a place to have fika

fikasugen — to have a fika craving

en kopp fika — a cup of coffee

welcome friends coming for fika or their own bread for afternoon sandwiches. While neither of us is a professional baker, we have both baked a lot from an early age. Through the years we have baked the classics and developed a few of our own recipes, and now we're collecting them all in this book.

For us, baking from scratch is simply the norm. We can't trace all of this to our roots, but there's something about baking and cooking with whole ingredients that feels inherently European: the appreciation for simple, good ingredients. You would be hard pressed to find any boxed baking mixes in a Swedish pantry.

The root of this book lies in the desire to make your own, and if you don't make your own, it's the desire to eat well: the feeling that when you can't bake your own cinnamon rolls for fika, you know a good local bakery that can. Extraordinary baked goods come about not only because the bakers know what they're doing but also because they are artists, paying close attention to the ingredients and materials they use. They are crafting a work of art with passion and soul.

Sweden being a country of the North, butter, potatoes, and milk have always been in abundance, while more exotic ingredients are a much more recent addition to the Swedish pantry. Today's Sweden, just like the rest of the Western world, has seen the influence of the supermarket and the variety of choice that it brings. And while you can get tomatoes year-round and processed foods are available like never before, there is still an inherent appreciation for good, wholesome ingredients in Swedish culture.

That doesn't mean that everyone only buys or bakes with the best ingredients all the time, but there is certainly a cultural respect for simplicity. After all, this is the land of dense bread thickly spread with butter. And while prebaked and store-bought goods are served for fika, particularly in the modern age of busy work schedules, homemade is still paramount.

The ideal of homemade is at the heart of this book. In fact, it is the essence of every single recipe. While we have modernized many of the recipes so that they're easy for even the beginner baker, the book isn't about speeding up the baking process and taking shortcuts. Some recipes are easy to whip up in 10 minutes, others you have to let sit for 24 hours. In our own kitchens, you will find organic sugar, real butter, and eggs from humanely raised chickens, because we believe that if you skimp on the ingredients and go for something of midrange quality, you can expect the same from your baked goods. Come into either one of our kitchens and you won't find an assortment of electrical gadgets. We bake as minimally as possible, making use of what we have.

Many of these recipes aren't complex, but they stand out because they are made with real ingredients. It might seem silly to crush your cardamom in a mortar and pestle instead of buying the ground version, and you might tire of kneading your dough by hand, but these are the details that we love and that make our recipes truly "handmade."

Just as much as fika is a reminder to take a moment to slow down and take a break, this book is a reminder to do things as basically and simply as possible. You don't have to be an expert to use this book, just someone who finds joy in the simplicity of good food. Use whole ingredients, nothing processed. Mix and knead by hand. Put love into the food you're making.

stocking the fika pantry

You will find that most fika recipes are renditions on a very standard baking combination of flour, sugar, butter, and eggs. There are spices here and there, and different ratios to be dealt with, but most of the time essential Swedish baking recipes boil down to those four ingredients.

This is good news for you the baker: although a lot of work has been put into the recipes in this book, and we have focused on creating new spins on old classics, the best part about these recipes is that you should play a little. You'll find several recipes where we offer optional ingredients, and you are encouraged to try them out. Variations on classics are what will make these recipes, and in turn fika, your own.

But before we get there, let's cover the basics of what you'll find in most of the recipes on the following pages. First it's important to note that we use organic ingredients whenever possible, and there are a few staples when it comes to those ingredients.

FLOUR For the most part you'll find that recipes in this book use all-purpose flour. A few of the recipes also call for rye flour, which is commonly used in many Scandinavian breads. Whenever possible, use the highest-quality unbleached flour that you can afford.

SUGAR When it comes to sugar, we stick to natural cane sugar. Some of the recipes also use brown sugar. It's also good to keep a little turbinado or raw sugar on hand for sprinkling on top of baked goods.

BUTTER Butter is at the core of practically every recipe in this book, as it has always been a Swedish pantry staple. Our recipes are made using unsalted butter, and because of this, we often add in a little salt to the recipes. Feel free to use salted butter, but be sure to decrease the amount of salt in the recipe as needed.

EGGS There's nothing better than watching as the golden yolk of a cracked egg spills into the bowl. Good eggs will get you a long way, which is why we prefer as local and well raised as possible. When whipping eggs into a meringue, it's much easier when they are at room temperature, which is why this instruction is indicated in some of the recipes. For eggs stored in the refrigerator, just be sure to take them out a few hours in advance.

SPICES Swedish baked goods are known for having a little kick to them, and spices are essential to the fika pantry. The most common are cardamom and cinnamon, and in our own kitchens, the policy is that you can never have enough cardamom. Other typical Swedish spices that you will find in this book are

cardamom

cinnamon

caraway, anise, and ginger. As with any spice, the fresher the better, which is why we like to grind our own spices when possible instead of purchasing preground. In the case of cardamom, that means buying whole seeds, or buying pods and removing the seeds. The recipes in this book are written with that in mind in order to achieve the best flavor, but feel free to use preground spices if that's what works best for you; just be sure to adjust the amounts.

NUTS Almonds and hazelnuts are commonly used in Swedish baking. A few recipes in this book are completely devoted to either of these two nuts, and others incorporate just a hint. Buy raw nuts in bulk and store them in glass containers with lids so they won't lose their flavor. If you aren't going to use them right away, it's best to store nuts in the refrigerator.

ground almonds

DRIED FRUIT In a cold climate where for most of the year fresh produce is available in only limited quantities, it's no surprise that dried fruits are a Swedish staple; a way of keeping the tastes of warmer months all year long. Figs, prunes, and raisins are typical Swedish ingredients and make their way into many of the recipes in this book.

CHOCOLATE Both unsweetened cocoa powder and dark chocolate are prominent in Swedish baking, and they're both items to keep on hand if you plan to do a lot of fika baking. As with all ingredients, be sure to buy good quality. After all, you can never bake too many chocolate cakes or cookies.

dark chocolate

Swedish ingredients and alternatives

There are a few Swedish standards that are hard to come by outside of Scandinavian grocery stores. You have two options: go to a specialty store or online retailer (page 155) or get creative to replace them yourself.

PÄRLSOCKER (PEARL SUGAR) Pearl sugar is a coarse, white sugar that does not melt at high temperatures, which means it is often used for garnish on things like Cinnamon and Cardamom Buns (page 26), Märta's Sliced Chocolate Cookies (page 42), or Finnish Sticks (page 44). There is no real replacement for pärlsocker, but you can easily find it at specialty shops. In the recipes that call for pärlsocker, we have recommended alternative toppings such as turbinado sugar in the event that you can't get your hands on any.

VANILJSOCKER (VANILLA SUGAR) The consistency of baking powder, vanilla sugar is a common ingredient in a lot of Swedish baking recipes. It's hard to track down outside of Sweden and because of that, all of our recipes are adapted to use pure vanilla extract or vanilla bean, like in Classic Vanilla Sauce (page 87).

MANDELMASSA (ALMOND PASTE) Almond paste is an essential Swedish ingredient. In Sweden you can buy it in any grocery store, where it comes in a plastic tube, similar to premade cookie dough. You can sometimes find it in grocery stores outside of Sweden in the baking section, but because making almond paste is so easy, we have incorporated a homemade version into all of the recipes that call for it.

almond paste

SIRAP (SYRUP) Syrup is a common ingredient in the Swedish pantry, for cookies, cakes, and breads. There are two versions: *ljus sirap*, "golden syrup," and *mörk sirap*, "dark syrup." Ljus sirap can be equated to the American light corn syrup, although it is processed from sugar beets. Mörk sirap is similar to light molasses. We have altered our recipes not to use either of these syrups as they can be hard to get outside Sweden, but they are worth noting since they are staples of general Swedish baking.

the fika baking tools

Baking has been a part of Swedish culture for a very long time, and as such, mastering fika specialties doesn't require technologically advanced kitchen products; mostly everything in this book can be accomplished with a measuring cup, a bowl, a wooden spoon, a whisk, and some creativity. As a rule, we never mix dough and batters in a food processor or stand mixer, although both can be used. Aside from grinding nuts (for which a food processor is recommended) and whisking egg whites (which is easier with an electric mixer), most of the recipes can be done completely by hand. That being said, there are a few tools that can be very helpful.

ROLLING PIN A rolling pin is an essential for rolled cookies like Swedish Gingersnaps (page 118), but you can get by without one if you have an empty wine bottle on hand. Not ideal, but it will do the trick.

SERRATED KNIFE For cutting breads, particularly the denser Scandinavian ones, a serrated knife is very useful. It's also helpful for many of the sliced cookies in this book, which are cut right after they come out of the oven and don't cut as easily with a regular knife.

PASTRY BRUSH For applying egg glazes, a pastry brush is indispensable. If you are looking to buy one, the silicone ones are a bit easier to clean, but you can even use a (clean!) paintbrush as an inexpensive option.

SPATULA Scraping out all those bowls, and getting to lick the leftover batter in the process, is much easier with a spatula on hand. We recommend the silicone spatulas that can also be used to stir ingredients over heat.

PASTRY CUTTER Known in Swedish as a *sporre*, this handled tool with a thin, sharp wheel is used for cutting pastry dough, similar to a pizza cutter.

PASTRY BLENDER A pastry blender with its curved
stainless steel blades makes it easy to cream butter and
sugar together by hand.

CHEESE SLICER While Americans are known to use knives to slice
cheese, Swedes would never dream of such a thing. You won't need this
tool for any baking, but when you want a little thinly sliced cheese and
jam on top of one of your freshly baked breads or rolls, the *osthyvel* is
your new best friend.

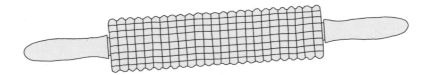

KRUSKAVEL What looks like a textured rolling pin is called a *kruskavel*
in Swedish, used in particular for making Crispbread Crackers (page 152)
and Swedish Flatbread (page 134). This is a very typical Swedish device,
not often found outside Scandinavia. However, you can easily use a fork
to do the same trick and create a beautiful textured design.

DOUGH SCRAPER Because many of the kinds of dough in this book are kneaded out on a flat surface, like a kitchen counter-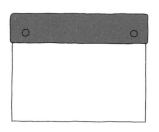top or table, a dough scraper is useful in cleaning up the parts that can stick to it. There are two kinds that we find useful. The steel version, which is flat and sharp, is great for scraping off sticky dough bits when you are finished kneading and working the dough. The plastic version, which is soft and has a rounded edge, is good for mixing dough and scraping the edges of the bowl in which you are making the dough.

MORTAR AND PESTLE For crushing whole spices, a mortar and pestle is very handy and gives you more spice flavor in your finished product, as compared to using an electric grinder, because of the chewable bits of spice seeds that remain. If you don't have a mortar and pestle, you can grind your seeds in a spice grinder or a coffee grinder, but grind them coarsely to achieve the same texture you would get from the mortar and pestle.

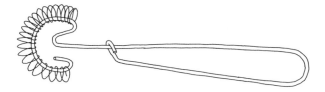

WHISK A step up from using a fork, a whisk helps you get your eggs nice and frothy when you beat them. For beating egg whites, we recommend a hand mixer, but in a pinch you can whisk by hand. A mixer makes it easier to achieve the stiffness of egg whites needed in some recipes.

NUT GRINDER Because of the amount of almond-based recipes in Swedish baking, it's no surprise that a nut grinder is called a *mandelkvarn*, which means "almond mill." A staple in many Swedish kitchens, a classic nut grinder can be hard to find elsewhere. You can get around this by processing almonds and other nuts in a food processor. This doesn't give exactly the consistency and fluffiness of a nut grinder, but it will work (see Grinding Nuts, opposite). We find that in most recipes it's nice to have a coarser meal with small pieces of nuts in it.

SILICONE BAKING MAT Many of the crisp cookies in this book are much easier baked on parchment paper, so to reduce waste, consider investing in a silicone baking mat. It removes parchment paper from the equation and keeps you from having to grease your baking sheets; you will soon wonder how you ever survived without one.

methods

There are a few specific methods that we use throughout our recipes. We have detailed them here so that you know what you're getting yourself into before you begin baking, and so that you have an easy-to-understand reference point.

MEASURING Quantities are provided in both volume and weight measurements. Choose whichever method you prefer.

CRUSHING SPICE SEEDS The recipes in this book use a lot of spices; you'll find that for many of them, the recipes ask for whole seeds, crushed. The best way to crush seeds, like anise and cardamom, is to use a mortar and pestle, spice grinder, or even a coffee grinder. Grind until coarsely ground, so you still have a few bits of the seeds. No mortar and pestle and no coffee grinder? Go the old route of placing seeds in a ziplock bag, or folding into a tea towel, and bashing on a flat, sturdy surface with a hammer. If you choose to skip using home-crushed seeds entirely and replace them with preground, be sure to slightly reduce the amount of spice in the recipe. Start small and taste-test as you go along.

GRINDING NUTS Many of the recipes in this book that involve nuts, like almonds and hazelnuts, call for grinding them. The traditional method for this is to use a nut grinder (opposite), but if you don't have one on hand, a food processor will work. The recipes that use this method will specify the consistency, be it finely ground, almost finely ground, or coarsely ground. When a recipe calls for finely ground, you want a light and fluffy consistency, almost the same as flour. For nuts ground almost finely ground, there should be an even consistency, but with very small pieces of nuts in the ground mixture. When a recipe calls for coarsely ground, you should have coarse pieces of nuts in the ground mixture, which can also be achieved through chopping by hand.

USING YEAST Although in Sweden most people bake with fresh yeast, we have adapted these recipes to use active dry yeast. You will find instructions for dissolving and correctly using yeast in the recipes.

The general, method is to dissolve the yeast in a few tablespoons of luke-warm liquid (warm to the touch) to "proof" the yeast and ensure it's still active, in which case it bubbles up in the warm liquid. Fresh yeast or instant yeast can also be used in these recipes, but be sure to adapt the amount accordingly.

FREEZING DOUGH If you are making cookies and don't want to bake the entire batch at one time, you can put the dough in the freezer and take it out when you're ready to bake again. This works great for dough that is sliced or rolled out, like Finnish Sticks (page 44) or Swedish Gingersnaps (page 118). To freeze the dough, roll it into a log, tightly wrap it in plastic wrap, and place it in an airtight freezer bag.

GREASING AND FLOURING PANS In Sweden, cake pans are greased and then sprinkled with fine bread crumbs, especially those recipes made in Bundt pans. This makes for a nice texture on the outside of cakes. When baking cake recipes in this book, feel free to employ this method, or just sprinkle in a little flour after you have greased the pan.

COOLING BAKED GOODS Many of the recipes in this book end up making a lot of cookies; as opposed to using a cooling rack, which may not fit all of the cookies, it's easiest to remove them from the baking sheet and cool them directly on the counter. Many of the cookies are also quite small in size, giving them a tendency to fall through cooling racks. Any flat surface will work, like a kitchen table. In some recipes, it's helpful to have air circulating around the baked goods, in which case a cooling rack is needed and we have specified.

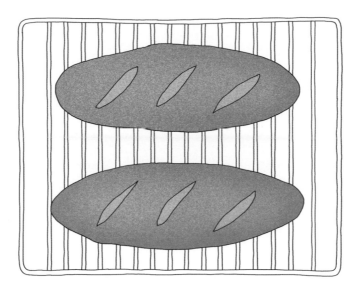

BAKING WITH PAPER LINERS In Sweden, paper liners are often used for a variety of baked goods, from cookies to cinnamon buns, but that doesn't mean that they are baked in a muffin tin. When paper liners are specified, you can simply place them directly out on a baking sheet and then place whichever dough or batter you are using in them.

CHAPTER 1

a history of Swedish coffee

t o say that Sweden, with a landmass of over 173,000 square miles and a population of about 9.5 million people, is a country of the North would of course be an understatement. Its northernmost tip lies above the Arctic Circle, and even when you're "down south," you're still at approximately the same latitude as Moscow. This is certainly no climate for growing tropical goods like coffee.

How, then, did this country become such a consumer of the drink born from a little dark bean that flourishes in warmer climates? In terms of cups per day, the Scandinavian countries top the list of global coffee consumers, drinking over 39 gallons/150 liters per person in one single year. You'd be hard pressed to find a Swede who doesn't enjoy a cup of coffee at least once a day, and while in some households tea may be the preferred morning drink, the Swedish coffee break has existed essentially since coffee came to Sweden.

Coffee officially made its way to Sweden in 1685, the first year that a mention of coffee is found in customs documents from Gothenburg, noting that someone had in fact imported a half kilo of beans. Three years later, coffee was available for purchase at the pharmacy. Through the 1700s the importation of coffee grew—King Charles XII himself was said to have brought a coffeemaker from Turkey back to Sweden—but coffee drinking was restricted to men. The original *kaffehus* (coffeehouses) of the era originated in port towns and were visited by sailors and the like; in fact, there was a time when even the word kaffehus was avoided, as it had an unsavory connotation.

Eventually, like much of the rest of Europe, the kaffehus became meeting places for intellectuals and politicians, and coffee culture was in turn equated with the upper echelons of society. As coffee drinking grew, so did the desire to restrain it. King Gustav III was convinced of coffee's negative health effects and that coffeehouse gatherings could be fodder for antimonarch sentiments, and was also against the drink for economic reasons, given that it was an expensive, imported luxury good. Coffee ended up being outlawed during his rule, but when people can't have a certain luxury item, they're sure to crave more of it, and coffee consumption grew.

In the 1800s, coffeehouses were overtaken by the classic *konditori*, a combination coffeehouse and patisserie. Here the sweet baked goods were just as important as the coffee that was served, and an outing to the local *kondis*, as konditori is often called for short, became a popular Sunday excursion. This was something that you dressed up for and that was considered a special event, a tradition that is very much at the root of today's popular café and fika culture.

It was around the same time that coffee became a common drink at home, the beverage of politicos and farmers alike. Soon it became a reason for a social gathering, and somewhere along the way the concept of fika was born. It's no surprise that in Swedish, you often refer to sweet breads as *kaffebröd*, or "coffee bread." Coffee and baked goods have gone hand in hand for over a century.

what are you drinking out of?

On a visit to your grandmother in Sweden, even if it is just a casual afternoon affair, the nice porcelain coffee cups will come out. This comes from a tradition of the older generation, who always had matching sets of cups, saucers, cookie plates, and a porcelain coffeepot to use when company came to visit. Fika was an honored time of day, and the servingware reflected that, so a beautiful, complete set was considered as essential to fika as a homemade baked good.

Until the last couple of decades, when more casual coffee culture made its way into Swedish territory, this is how coffee was consumed. Any afternoon coffee gathering, be it at a church or someone's home, would feature a beautiful porcelain set, as indicative of fika as the English tradition of tea. The typical Swedish method of brewing coffee in the earlier days was *kokkaffe*. This "cooked coffee" is made by placing water and coarse coffee grounds in a kettle and boiling. Because of brewing it in this way, the coffee was often scalding hot, so it was common to pour a little of the coffee from the cup directly onto the saucer and drink it from there. Swedes call this *dricka på fat*, essentially, "drink from the saucer." Alongside the coffee, you would always find a pitcher of cream and a bowl of sugar cubes, which were often taken with the help of silver tongs. The sugar was put between the teeth and the coffee consumed through it, in Swedish called *dricka kaffe på bit*, literally, "drink coffee on the sugar cube"—a truly vintage style of fika.

Another Swedish coffee tradition that dates to this era is the *kaffegök*, also known as *kaffekask*, a blend of coffee and alcohol, simply made by adding approximately a shot glass of vodka to a cup of coffee.

Perhaps the most well-known visual of the Swedish coffee break are the cups and saucers that Swedish designer Stig Lindberg did for

Gustavsberg. The simple lines and patterns of the many Swedish designers of the 1950s and '60s have inspired hundreds of variations and unique designs, and have made the original cups the proverbial pot of gold for vintage lovers. Nothing symbolizes the traditional Swedish kitchen of the era like these cups.

Even today, using the classic cup and saucer combination heightens the fika experience and gives it an element of celebration. At a Swedish dinner party, an after-dinner cup of coffee is sure to be served in a traditional *mockakopp*, a smaller version of the porcelain cup and saucer.

seven kinds of cookies

With the rise of the konditori, coffee in Sweden became synonymous with what it was served with; if people were invited over for coffee, it was practically a social expectation to have something delicious to pair it with. In the middle of the 1900s, the *kafferep* became a commonplace affair for birthdays, funerals, or just a good reason for older ladies to meet and socialize. Similar to fika, a kafferep is a larger and more formal gathering.

The social rules require that a true kafferep include small cookies, buns, and a version of sponge cake. For a bigger celebration, you would even add a torte to the mix. The idea is to always have an abundance of treats.

The cookies of these classic social gatherings are called *småkakor*, literally "small cookies." Often made from a basic form of sugar cookie dough, what distinguishes småkakor is that they are small and sweet, and you can always expect a variety of them on hand at any typical coffee gathering. In fact, the traditional *kakfat*, or tiered set of cookie plates that was common at these gatherings, was meant to be filled with a variety of *småkakor*. Any good hostess would bake these from scratch, a tradition borne out by the name of one of Sweden's oldest and most classic cookbooks, *Sju Sorters Kakor*, or *Seven Kinds of Cookies*. Today the book is a staple in any Swede's cookbook collection. And while serving up seven kinds of cookies takes a certain level of ambition and commitment, the concept is ingrained into the Swedish mind-set.

But you never know when someone will arrive and need to be served a cup of coffee, and for that reason, throughout the decades cookies have most commonly been stored in decorative cookie tins. Nowadays, you'll also find a batch in the freezer, particularly if they are butter based. Because in Sweden, when there's company, you serve coffee; and serving coffee without something to eat alongside is simply unthinkable.

recipes

As coffee flowed into Swedish culture, a handful of recipes soon became staples for coffee gatherings. From Cinnamon Buns (page 26) to Cardamom Cake (page 30), these are some of the most iconic and traditional Swedish fika recipes, including several of our favorite småkakor, with a few alterations here and there to make them truly stand out.

vetebullar

CINNAMON AND CARDAMOM BUNS

makes 30 to 36 buns, or 2 lengths

Bullar (buns) are perhaps the quintessential component to a Swedish coffee break, and *vete* in Swedish means "wheat." Vetebullar is therefore the general term for wheat-based dough that can be turned into any number of bun creations. *Kanelbullar* (cinnamon buns) and *kardemummabullar* (cardamom buns) are common variations on this type of bun, and while the traditional "roll" form is common, there are twisted varieties as well. Typically they are baked and served in paper liners. Kanelbullar are such an iconic pastry that an entire day in Sweden is devoted to them (October 4, for those considering celebrating).

This recipe has both filling varieties, and once you've mastered the dough, you can start experimenting with your own fillings. If a Swede knows one thing, it's this: no matter what the variation, bullar are always best fresh out of the oven, and make for a wonderful-smelling kitchen.

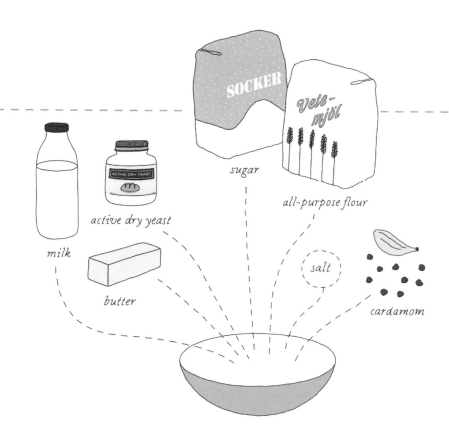

milk

active dry yeast

butter

sugar

all-purpose flour

salt

cardamom

dough

7 tablespoons (3.5 ounces, 99 grams) unsalted butter

1½ cups (360 milliliters) milk

2 teaspoons active dry yeast

4½ cups (1⅜ pounds, 638 grams) all-purpose flour

¼ cup (1.75 ounces, 50 grams) natural cane sugar

1½ teaspoons whole cardamom seeds, crushed

¼ teaspoon salt

To prepare the dough, melt the butter in a saucepan; then stir in the milk. Heat until warm to the touch (about 110°F/43°C). In a small bowl, dissolve the yeast in 2 to 3 tablespoons of the warm mixture. Stir and let sit for a few minutes until bubbles form on top of the yeast.

In a large bowl, mix together the flour, sugar, cardamom, and salt. Add the yeast mixture along with the remaining butter and milk. Work together with your hands until you can make the dough into a ball.

CONTINUED

Transfer the dough to a flat surface and knead it until smooth and elastic, 3 to 5 minutes. The dough should feel moist, but if it sticks to your fingers add a tiny bit of flour. The dough is fully kneaded when you slice into it with a sharp knife and see small air bubbles throughout. Return the dough to the bowl, cover with a clean tea towel, and place in a draft-free place to rise until doubled in size, about 1 hour.

Grease a baking sheet, or place medium paper liners directly on the sheet.

Make the filling right before the dough has finished rising. Using a fork, cream the butter together with the sugar and the spices until you get an evenly mixed, spreadable paste.

When the dough has finished rising, take half of the dough and place it on a flat surface. Roll it out with a rolling pin to an 11 by 17-inch (28 by 43-centimeter) rectangle. Place the rectangle on the surface so that the long side is closest to you.

Carefully spread half of the filling on top of the rolled-out dough so that it covers the entire area; be sure to go all the way to the edges. Begin at the long side near you and roll the dough upward (see diagram). Slice the roll into 15 to 18 equally sized slices and place them, rolled side up, on the baking sheet or in the paper liners. If using a baking sheet, pinch the ends of the slices to keep them from pulling away during baking. Repeat with the second half of the dough. Cover the buns with a clean tea towel and let rise for 45 minutes.

filling

7 tablespoons (3.5 ounces, 99 grams) unsalted butter, room temperature

½ cup (3.5 ounces, 99 grams) natural cane sugar

3 to 4 teaspoons ground cinnamon or whole cardamom seeds, crushed

2 additional teaspoons crushed cardamom seeds, if making filling using cinnamon

topping

1 egg, beaten

Pearl sugar or chopped almonds

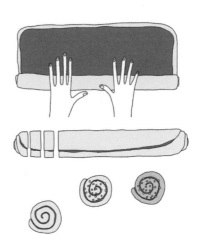

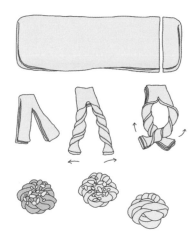

Preheat the oven to 435°F (225°C).

When the buns have risen, carefully brush them with the beaten egg and sprinkle each with the pearl sugar.

Bake for 8 to 10 minutes. If you are baking a length, bake for an additional 10 minutes. Remove from the oven, transfer the buns from the baking sheet to the counter, and cover with a tea towel to cool. Serve freshly baked, and if not eaten right away, store in the freezer once they are completely cooled.

VARIATIONS Instead of rolling the dough to make the classic bun shape, you can also make twists (see diagram above), a common formation when making cardamom buns, as well as baking a length and cutting a design into the dough with scissors to let the filling ooze out a little (see below).

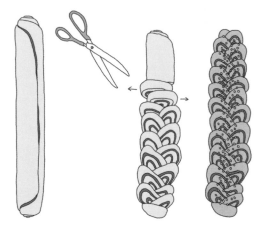

kardemummakaka

CARDAMOM CAKE

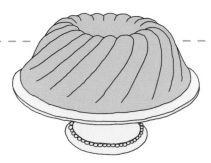

makes one 6-cup Bundt cake

For those outside of Sweden, the mention of cardamom may inspire thoughts of India or the Middle East, but anyone with Swedish heritage will immediately taste their homeland when they bite into something sweet with a hint of cardamom. Cardamom may come from the other side of the world, but Swedes are huge consumers of the spice, and it shows in Swedish baking. In our humble fika opinion, you can never have too much cardamom.

This cardamom cake, inspired by a recipe from Johanna's mother, Mona, is a basic, fluffy and moist cake with just the right amount of spice. While cardamom has a strong flavor no matter how you use it, we prefer the crushed version. You get the most flavor out of the seeds that way, and you end up with small crunchy bits of cardamom in the cake.

10½ tablespoons (5.25 ounces, 148 grams) unsalted butter

3 egg yolks, room temperature

¼ cup (1.88 ounces, 53 grams) firmly packed brown sugar

¾ cup (3.75 ounces, 106 grams) all-purpose flour

4 teaspoons whole cardamom seeds, crushed

3 tablespoons lemon juice

¼ teaspoon salt

3 egg whites, room temperature

¾ cup (5.25 ounces, 148 grams) natural cane sugar

Preheat the oven to 350°F (175°C). Grease and flour a Bundt pan.

In a saucepan, melt the butter. Remove from the heat and set aside to cool.

In a bowl, whisk together the egg yolks and the brown sugar until frothy. Pour the slightly cooled butter into the egg yolk and sugar mixture and whisk together a little longer. Sift the flour, then stir it carefully into the batter along with the cardamom, lemon juice, and salt. Stirring as little as possible, work the ingredients together until you get a smooth, even batter.

In a separate bowl, whisk the egg whites, ideally with an electric mixer. When soft peaks form, add the cane sugar little by little. Whisk until stiff peaks form. Carefully fold the sugar and egg white mixture into the batter and keep folding until the batter is evenly blended. Be careful not to overstir. Pour directly into the Bundt pan.

Bake for 40 to 45 minutes. The cake is done when a knife or toothpick comes out clean when inserted at the thickest part of the cake. If the cake starts to get a golden brown color earlier (which can happen after 20 minutes), remove it from the oven, cover it with aluminum foil, and put back in the oven. This will prevent the top of the cake from burning.

Remove the cake from the oven and let cool for a bit before inverting it onto a plate.

apelsinsnittar

ORANGE ALMOND SLICES

makes 48 cookies

Many Swedish cookie recipes start with the butter, sugar, and flour base, and while that's delicious, it can quickly get boring. This recipe, however, puts the classic dough to more interesting use: holding a delicious almond filling that has just a hint of orange zest, and topping it with a citrusy icing. These distinctive cookies look beautiful served alongside classic porcelain cups of fresh coffee. They store well in the freezer, so keep some on hand for when company unexpectedly arrives.

To prepare the dough, in a large bowl, cream together the butter and sugar until well blended. Add the flour, egg yolk, and ginger. Work the mixture together with your hands until the dough can be formed into a ball. Cover and let sit in the refrigerator for 30 minutes.

When ready to bake, preheat the oven to 400°F (200°C). Grease a baking sheet or line it with parchment paper or a silicone baking mat

To prepare the filling, mix the almonds, sugar, and almond extract in a food processor until the ingredients come together; depending on how dry the almonds are, you will get a sticky to smooth consistency.

dough

10 tablespoons (5 ounces, 142 grams) unsalted butter, room temperature

½ cup (3.5 ounces, 99 grams) natural cane sugar

1½ cups (7.5 ounces, 213 grams) all-purpose flour

1 egg yolk

2 teaspoons ground ginger

filling

1½ cups (7.5 ounces, 213 grams) blanched almonds

½ cup (3.5 ounces, 99 grams) natural cane sugar

1 teaspoon pure almond extract

1 egg white

Zest of 1 medium-size orange, 1 to 2 tablespoons

icing

¼ cup (1 ounce, 28 grams) confectioners' sugar

1 to 2 teaspoons orange juice

In a bowl, whisk the egg white until frothy. Mix in the almond mixture and the orange zest.

Divide the dough into 4 equal parts. On a floured surface, roll each part with a rolling pin into a rectangle, about 10 by 4 inches (25.5 by 10 centimeters), with the longest side toward you. It is easiest to roll out the dough between 2 sheets of plastic wrap.

For each rectangle of dough, use a quarter of the filling, spreading it lengthwise down the middle of the rectangle, parallel to the longest side. This should take up the middle third of the dough, leaving one third of uncovered dough at the top and bottom edges. Fold the top third down so that it completely covers the filling, then fold the bottom third up to meet the top, as if folding a piece of paper into thirds. If any of the dough breaks in the process of folding, pinch it together with your fingers so that the filling doesn't leak out. Pinch the ends of the log closed. Repeat this process for each log.

When transferring to the baking sheet, carefully turn the logs over so that the folded section is on the bottom. Bake for 15 minutes, until the edges are lightly browned. Remove from the oven and let cool on the baking sheet.

To prepare the icing, mix together the confectioners' sugar and just enough orange juice to give a thin,

CONTINUED

smooth consistency. Add the orange juice slowly so the icing doesn't become too runny.

When the cookie logs are cool, carefully transfer them to a cutting board. Drizzle the icing over the top of each log or spread it on the logs using a spatula. Let the icing set for a few minutes before cutting each log into 12 equally sized slices.

When cooled, store in an airtight container. These cookies also store well in the freezer.

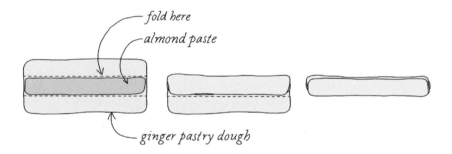

fold here

almond paste

ginger pastry dough

havreflarn med choklad

OAT CRISP CHOCOLATE SANDWICH COOKIES

makes 16 sandwich cookies or 32 halves

Havreflarn is a traditional Swedish recipe that often gets revamped in different ways, most notably with chocolate; dip it, drizzle it, or squeeze a layer in between two cookies. A sandwich cookie is always more fun, right? The crispy and sweet oat texture pairs well with chocolate, so in this version, we went for a sandwich cookie, with just a hint of ginger. You can, of course, skip the sandwiching and just serve the cookies plain.

cookies

1½ cups (5.25 ounces, 148 grams) rolled oats

1 tablespoon all-purpose flour

1 teaspoon baking powder

1 egg

½ cup (3.5 ounces, 99 grams) natural cane sugar

7 tablespoons (3.5 ounces, 99 grams) unsalted butter

filling

4 ounces (113 grams) 60% bittersweet chocolate

1 teaspoon ground ginger

Preheat the oven to 350°F (175°C). Line a baking sheet with parchment paper (or use a silicone baking mat).

In a food processor, pulse the oats into a coarse meal. You want a little bit of texture, so don't grind them all the way. If you don't have a food processor, use the smallest oats you can find, to make for a better cookie consistency.

In a large bowl, mix the flour and baking powder.

In a separate bowl, whisk together the egg and sugar until frothy. All of the sugar should be dissolved

CONTINUED

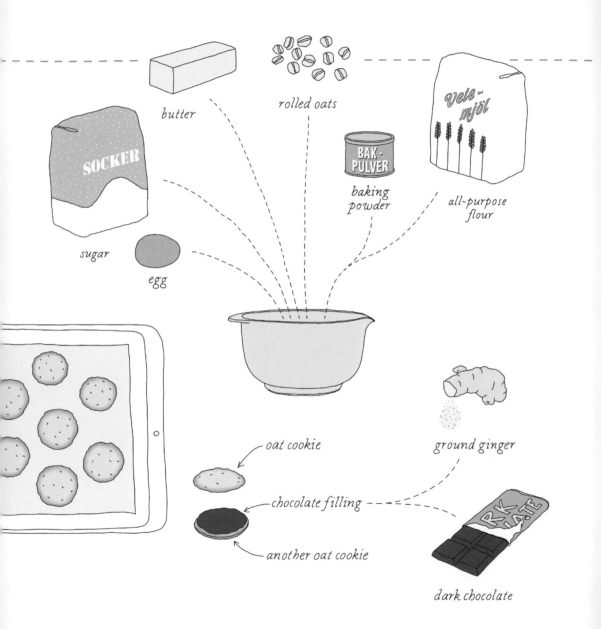

butter

rolled oats

vetemjöl

SOCKER

sugar

egg

BAK-PULVER

baking powder

all-purpose flour

oat cookie

ground ginger

chocolate filling

another oat cookie

dark chocolate

and the batter should have a light color. Stir the flour and baking powder into the batter until well blended.

In a small saucepan, melt the butter. Remove from the heat and stir in the oats with a fork until the oats are completely covered with the melted butter. Add the oats to the batter and stir until well blended.

Spoon the batter by about 2-teaspoon portions onto the baking sheet, leaving 2 inches (5 centimeters) between each cookie. Use your fingers to lightly press and flatten each cookie.

Bake for 6 to 10 minutes, until the edges of the cookies are golden brown.

Remove from the oven and let cool on the baking sheet until the cookies have hardened; then remove the cookies from the sheet and place on the counter. Make sure the edges are not touching one another or the cookies will get soft. Let cool completely.

To prepare the filling, slowly melt the chocolate in the top of a double boiler or in a clean heatproof bowl placed in a saucepan of barely simmering water. Stir the ginger into the melted chocolate.

Spread the chocolate mixture on the flat side of one cookie and place another cookie on top, sandwiching them together. Set the sandwiched cookies back on the counter and let sit until the chocolate has hardened.

Store in an airtight container to keep the cookies crisp.

fikonrutor

FIG SQUARES

makes 35 squares

A soft, buttery dough and a fruity jam: it comes as no surprise that the standard recipe for fruit squares is popular in Sweden. Most often baked with raspberry jam, this version uses Fig Preserves (page 146). It can also be made with other kinds of firmly set jam. The recipe is adapted from a newspaper clipping Johanna found in her mother Mona's recipe drawer.

In a food processor, finely grind the almonds.

Place all of the flour directly on a flat surface or in a large bowl. Add the almonds and blend the two together well with your hands. Make a hole in the middle and add the sugar, butter, and egg. Work quickly with your fingertips (or with a knife) to form into a dough. Cover the dough and let sit in the refrigerator for an hour or more.

Preheat the oven to 400°F (200°C). Grease a baking sheet or line it with parchment paper or a silicone baking mat.

Take two-thirds of the dough and roll it out with a rolling pin to a 9 by 13-inch (23 by 33-centimeter) rectangle (make sure it will fit on your baking sheet), a little less than ¼ inch (.5 centimeter) thick. It is

½ cup (2.5 ounces, 71 grams) raw almonds

1½ cups (7.5 ounces, 213 grams) all-purpose flour

⅔ cup (4.67 ounces, 132 grams) natural cane sugar

¾ cup (6 ounces, 170 g) unsalted butter, chilled and cut into small pieces

1 egg, beaten

About 1⅓ cups (320 milliliters) Fig Preserves (page 146), or store-bought fig jam (firmly set)

easiest to roll out the dough between 2 sheets of plastic wrap. Place the rectangle on the baking sheet. Spread the preserves on top of the dough, covering the entire rectangle.

Roll out the rest of the dough using the same method and to the same thickness. Using a pastry cutter or knife, cut the dough into ⅜-inch- (1-centimeter-) wide strips. Crisscross the strips diagonally, creating a lattice top.

Bake for about 10 minutes. Remove from the oven; while still warm, cut into 35 equal squares. Separate the squares from each other so that the edges are not touching and let them cool.

Store the squares in an airtight container.

rolled out dough, 9"x 13"

fig preserves

about ⅜" wide strips of dough

when baked, cut out about 35 squares

syltgrottor

JAM THUMBPRINT COOKIES

makes 24 cookies

A buttery cookie is one thing, but a buttery cookie filled with jam is quite another, and this recipe will brighten up any cookie platter; use a different kind of jam and vary not only the taste but also the color. A little different from American thumbprint cookies, the Swedish version is baked directly in small paper liners and is a little lighter and softer, as well as a little more buttery. In fact, directly translated, the name *syltgrottor* means "jam caves."

This recipe has crushed anise seeds added to the dough, which is a nice spice to complement the raspberries and blueberries in the Queen's Jam (page 91) that serves as the filling. In a pinch, if you don't have jam on hand, you can crush fresh blueberries and mix them with a few tablespoons of sugar.

2 cups (10 ounces, 284 grams) all-purpose flour

½ cup (3.5 ounces, 99 grams) natural cane sugar

1 teaspoon baking powder

2 teaspoons anise seed, crushed

14 tablespoons (7 ounces, 198 grams) unsalted butter, chilled

½ teaspoon vanilla extract

About ½ cup (120 milliliters) Queen's Jam (page 91)

Preheat the oven to 400°F (200°C). Spread 24 small paper liners out directly on a baking sheet.

Mix together the flour, sugar, baking powder, and anise seed. Add the butter in small pieces and work together with your hands. Mix in the vanilla and work the dough until you can make it into a ball.

Form the dough into 24 small balls. You can do this with the help of a tablespoon—the balls should be about the size of walnuts—or roll the dough into a log, slice into 24 pieces, and roll each piece into a ball. Place the balls in the small paper liners.

Push your thumb into the center of each cookie, making a little crater. Put a small spoonful of the jam into each crater.

Bake for 10 to 12 minutes, until the cookies are a light golden brown. Remove from the oven and let cool.

Store the cookies in an airtight container.

märtas skurna chokladkakor

MÄRTA'S SLICED CHOCOLATE COOKIES

makes 48 cookies

Sliced cookies are a common classic in the Swedish kitchen, most likely because it's a very simple way to make a good-looking cookie. Just roll, bake, and slice and you have fika ready in less than no time. While many Swedish småkakor recipes build off of the same basic butter dough, this one has the excellent addition of chocolate. The original recipe comes from the iconic Swedish cookbook *Sju Sorters Kakor*, but ours has just a little extra chocolate in it, made particularly for anyone who has a love of that deep, dark, delicious chocolate taste.

Traditionally, these cookies are topped with pearl sugar (see page 9), which makes for a beautiful white scattering on top of the dark brown slices. If you can't get pearl sugar, substitute a bit of turbinado sugar for an extra crunch on top of the cookie.

dough

1 cup (8 ounces, 227 grams) unsalted butter, room temperature

1⅓ cups (9.34 ounces, 264 grams) natural cane sugar

2 eggs

2 teaspoons pure vanilla extract

2 cups (10 ounces, 284 grams) all-purpose flour

¼ cup (.75 ounce, 21 grams) plus 2 tablespoons unsweetened cocoa powder

1 teaspoon baking powder

topping

1 egg, beaten

Pearl sugar

Cream together the butter and sugar. In a separate bowl, whisk 2 of the eggs. Add to the butter and sugar mixture along with the vanilla and mix until well blended.

In a separate bowl, mix together the flour, cocoa powder, and baking powder. Add the flour mixture to the butter and sugar mixture and work together until a dough forms.

Cover the dough and let sit in the refrigerator for at least 30 minutes.

Preheat the oven to 400°F (200°C). Grease a baking sheet or line it with parchment paper or a silicone baking mat.

Divide the dough into 4 equal parts and roll each part into a 12-inch (30.5-centimeter) log. Place the logs on the baking sheet (you can also form the logs directly on the baking sheet to begin with), leaving at least 2 inches between each log. Press the logs so that they flatten out to about 2 inches (5 centimeters) wide and a little less than ½ inch (1.5 centimeters) thick.

Brush each log with the beaten egg. Sprinkle with the pearl sugar.

Bake for 15 minutes. Remove the cookie logs from the oven; while still warm, cut each log diagonally into 12 equally sized slices. Place cookies on the counter and let cool completely.

Store in an airtight container.

finska pinnar

FINNISH STICKS

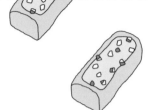

makes 40 cookies

Finska pinnar are a Swedish cookie classic, coming from, as the name insinuates, our neighbors to the east. It is reminiscent of old-time fika spreads at churches and social gatherings, when a specific number of cookies were always required. At such gatherings you would certainly have found Finska pinnar, a small cookie that should never be underrated. But don't feel bad if you only have time to make one kind of cookie; Finska pinnar will do the trick.

In a food processor, finely grind the almonds.

In a large bowl, cream together the butter and sugar until well blended. Add the flour, ground almonds, and almond extract. Work together with your hands until you can make the dough into a ball (if necessary, add ½ to 1 teaspoon water to help hold the dough together). Divide the dough into 4 equal parts and roll each part into a thick log, about 4 inches (10 centimeters) long. Wrap the logs in plastic wrap and let them sit in the fridge for about 30 minutes.

Preheat the oven to 350°F (175°C). Grease a baking sheet or line it with parchment paper or a silicone baking mat.

dough

½ cup (2.5 ounces, 71 grams) blanched almonds

10 tablespoons (5 ounces, 142 grams) unsalted butter, room temperature

⅓ cup (2.33 ounces, 66 grams) natural cane sugar

1½ cups (7.5 ounces, 213 grams) all-purpose flour

topping

¼ teaspoon pure almond extract

1 egg, beaten

Pearl sugar and/or chopped almonds

Roll out each log to about 20 inches (51 centimeters) long and slightly larger than ½ inch (1.5 centimeters) in diameter. If you need to, sprinkle a little flour on the surface to help rolling. Cut each log into 10 equally sized sections.

Place the cookies on the baking sheet. Carefully brush each cookie with the beaten egg before sprinkling with the pearl sugar and chopped almonds.

Bake for 10 to 12 minutes, until the cookies are a light golden brown. Remove the cookies from the oven and place them on the counter. Make sure the edges are not touching one another or the cookies will get soft. Let cool completely.

Store in an airtight container or in the freezer.

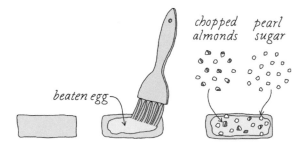

chopped almonds   pearl sugar

beaten egg

muskotsnittar

NUTMEG SLICES

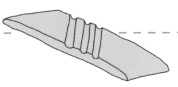

makes 40 cookies

Another sliced cookie, *muskotsnittar* is a hassle-free, spice-filled cookie that pairs well with coffee. Simple and very Swedish, the flavor makes it just as good for a holiday cookie as it is in the middle of the summer, and with a little linear decoration on the top, it's both beautiful and fun to eat. Thanks to the buttery consistency, these cookies also freeze well (and are even delicious eaten frozen!).

In a large bowl, mix together the sugar, cinnamon, nutmeg, and ginger. Add the butter to the sugar mixture and cream together until well blended. Mix in the flour and work together with your hands until you get a firm dough.

Cover the dough and let sit in the refrigerator for at least 30 minutes.

Preheat the oven to 350°F (175°C). Grease a baking sheet or line it with parchment paper or a silicone baking mat.

Divide the dough into 4 equal parts and roll each part into a log about 14 inches (35.5 centimeters) long. Place on a baking sheet (you should have

⅔ cup (5 ounces, 142 grams) firmly packed brown sugar

1 tablespoon ground cinnamon

1 teaspoon freshly grated nutmeg

1 teaspoon ground ginger

17 tablespoons (8.5 ounces, 241 grams) unsalted butter, room temperature

2 cups (10 ounces, 284 grams) all-purpose flour

room for 2 logs on 1 sheet) and flatten out to ¼ inch (0.5 centimeter) thick. Leave about 2 inches (5 centimeters) between the logs, as they will spread out a bit. Using the back of a fork, lightly press into the dough to create a linear design.

Bake the logs in 2 batches for 15 to 17 minutes, until the edges are golden brown. Remove from the oven and let cool for a few minutes on the baking sheet before cutting each log into 10 equally sized slices. Let the baking sheet cool before using it for the second batch. Let the slices cool completely.

Store in an airtight container.

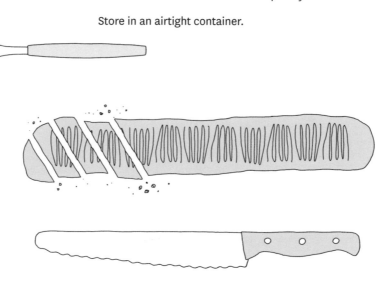

hasselnötsflarn

HAZELNUT CRISPS

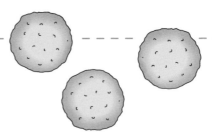

makes about 30 cookies

Crisp cookies are common in the Swedish kitchen because of their simplicity; if you're committed to serving the full range of cookies on your cookie platter, you can't spend too much time on each type of cookie. And these couldn't be easier: ground hazelnuts, sugar, butter, egg, and a touch of vanilla. Not only are they easy, but because they don't contain flour, they're also gluten-free. If you're not eating them with a cup of coffee, try them with ice cream.

Preheat the oven to 350°F (175°C). Line a baking sheet with a silicone baking mat or parchment paper.

In a saucepan, melt the butter. Remove from the heat and set aside.

In a food processor, grind the hazelnuts until almost finely ground.

In a bowl, whisk the egg until frothy, then stir in the sugar and vanilla. Pour in the slightly cooled butter and mix together until well blended. Add the hazelnuts and stir until an even batter forms.

¼ cup (2 ounces, 57 grams) unsalted butter

¾ cup (3.75 ounces, 106 grams) raw hazelnuts

1 egg

½ cup (3.5 ounces, 99 grams) natural cane sugar

½ teaspoon pure vanilla extract

Spoon the batter by 1-teaspoon drops onto the baking sheet, leaving 2 inches (5 centimeters) between each cookie. If you make them slightly larger, just be sure to flatten them with your fingertips so that they bake to an even crisp.

Bake for 8 to 10 minutes, until dark golden brown around the edges. Remove from the oven and let cool on the baking sheet until they are hard, then carefully transfer them to the counter.

When fully cooled, store in an airtight container to keep the cookies crisp.

CHAPTER 2

- - - - - - -

modern-day fika

in many places in the world, such as the United States, coffee is often equated with speed—we drink it to wake up, we grab a latte on the go, and if we need an afternoon pick-me-up, we reach for the office coffeepot that has been sitting on the "warm" setting all day.

In Sweden it's practically the opposite, more commonly representing a pause in the day, a time to slow down. Breaking for coffee is an excuse to enjoy a break from what you're doing; it's important to make time to enjoy life. Certainly, coffee is consumed for breakfast in many Swedish households, but a cup of coffee isn't just a means to waking up; it's an important moment in the day, be it at work or with friends on weekends. Life is for living, which means life is fueled by fika.

fika at work

In most Swedish office spaces you'll find a *fikarum*, the "fika room." This is the break room, often with a pantry and kitchen, intended for taking a fika break and also serving as the proverbial office water cooler. Coffee brings people together, and in Sweden fika—even at work—is a reason to socialize.

If you're a good coworker, you might even bring homemade kanelbullar to work one day. You're sure to have the favor returned the following week; a chance to see what someone else can do with cardamom. And when one of your coworkers shows up with fika goods purchased from the local supermarket, you can feel the home bakers raising their eyebrows in moderate disdain. Baking is such a part of Swedish culture that even the busiest of people will make time for a home-baked cinnamon bun or chocolate cake.

"ska vi fika?"

While coffee drinking is a long-standing Swedish tradition, the more northern custom of dark, black filter coffee served in porcelain cups has given way to the influences of southern European coffee culture, which tends to favor espresso drinks. While you will still find the classic konditori in Sweden, serving iconic cakes and fancy pastries in a more traditional setting, modern cafés are sleek in a Scandinavian minimal aesthetic (think lots of white walls, well-placed plants, and cool textile designs on the curtains) and cosmopolitan in their menus.

THE MEANING OF MYSIG

The Swedish word *mysig* loosely translates to "cozy," but the meaning is larger: a warm kitchen to welcome you inside after you've been out in the winter snow; Friday night curled up on the couch with a cup of tea; a cute café with big cups of coffee and oversize chairs. The goal is to create a moment that's mysig and, so often, mysig and fika go hand in hand.

The word is derived from *mysa*, which originally meant "to smile with contentedness" but has come to be used as a verb indicating enjoying, relaxing, and even cuddling. It's a good word, and you can see why it's a perfect partner to a warm drink like coffee or tea. Whether it's a rainy day in March or a sunny afternoon in July, creating a space that's mysig is almost as essential to enjoying your coffee as serving a delicious baked good. Sometimes it's the setting—the perfect spot on a granite cliff overlooking a lake. Other times it's the serving—your grandmother's antique set of porcelain coffee cups coming out in honor of someone's birthday. If you're going to do Swedish fika right, make sure it's mysig.

Kaffe lattes are the go-to drink of girlfriends out for an afternoon fika, and they pair well with oversize muffins piled in breadbaskets atop the café counter. Espresso, cappuccino, and even Chemex—you can find it all in a modern Swedish café. But the good old classic is still strong *bryggkaffe* (drip coffee), with *påtår*, the Swedish word for "refill," and you can always be sure that it will be dark and delicious every single time. As the Swedes love their coffee, it should come as no surprise that there's even a word for the third filling of the cup: *tretår*.

While coffee shops in the United States are filled with laptops and freelancers, doubling as remote office spaces where you can crouch for a few hours as long as you keep refilling your mug, cafés in Sweden are meeting points for friends. "Ska vi fika? " ("Shall we fika?") could just as well mean "let's check out a new café." In the winter you want something cozy, warm, and full of light. In the summer you want an inviting terrace, a carafe of water served with your coffee, and hopefully a summer berry tart with heavy whipped cream. Getting together over fika isn't just a time to catch up with an old friend; it's yet another reason to take a moment and appreciate the good life.

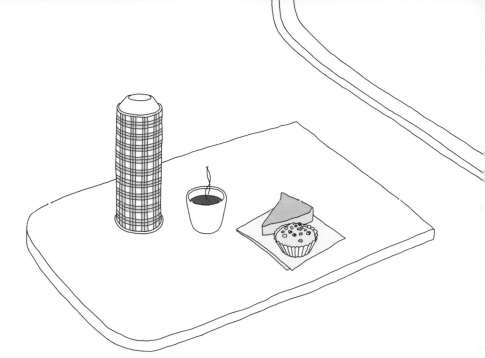

fika for traveling

As a Swede, one doesn't board a train or embark on a long car ride without thinking about fika. On the go, fika is part of the overall travel experience. Crossing Sweden on the rails, you're never without a bistro car offering up a fika special—a paper cup of coffee and a cinnamon bun for a few Swedish coins—but if you really want to live well, you'll be prepared and bring your own.

This goes for day trips as well. An afternoon at the beach in the summertime necessitates a thermos and a bag of baked goods. A winter outing of cross-country skiing requires the same. Forget granola and protein bars thrown into the bag at the last minute; packing fika to take with you is about bringing all the things you would consume inside and taking them outdoors.

Going out for fika is as much a part of Swedish culture as bringing your own, and while an afternoon hike in the forest certainly requires a backpack with a thermos, a baked good wrapped in tinfoil, and something to sit on, an excursion to a new city is the chance to check out a local café. From the countryside to the cosmopolitan hub of Stockholm, fika is a common affair. In the hinterlands of Värmland you may end up taking part in fika at an old farmhouse, recently opened for a summer exhibition of local handicrafts; in Malmö you will map out who makes the best semlor; and in downtown Gothenburg you'll crowd into a popular café to see if their chokladbollar are any better than the ones you make at home. Any place serving coffee will have an offering of goods to eat for fika, and they're always worth a try.

recipes

A combination of more modern-day baked goods inspired by cafés and recipes that have become the go-to goodies for a younger generation, this collection of recipes will take you from the office to a day on the train to an afternoon catch-up with friends.

mandelkaka

ALMOND TART

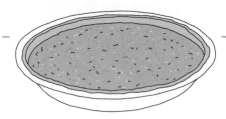

makes one 9-inch (23-centimeter) tart

Mazariner are a beloved Swedish recipe, small tartlets filled with almond paste and topped with icing. But they're a little time consuming to bake, and while Swedes are happy to snag one at a pastry shop, these are rarely made at home. This is where the almond tart comes in. It's the same concept—pastry dough and almonds—but much quicker and simpler to make. It's the kind of tart that's just as good with your afternoon cup of coffee as it is served as dessert at a dinner with friends.

To prepare the dough, in a large bowl, mix the flour and sugar. Add the butter in small cubes and work together with your hands until you get a coarse meal; then work in the egg yolk until you can make the dough into a ball. Form a round with the dough, wrap in plastic wrap, and let sit in the refrigerator for at least 30 minutes.

Preheat the oven to 350°F (175°C). Grease a 9-inch (23-centimeter) pie pan or springform baking pan.

To prepare the filling, melt the butter and set aside to cool.

dough

¾ cup (3.75 ounces, 106 grams) all-purpose flour

2 tablespoons natural cane sugar

5 tablespoons (2.5 ounces, 71 grams) unsalted butter

1 egg yolk

filling

4 tablespoons (2 ounces, 57 grams) butter

1 cup (5 ounces, 142 grams) raw almonds

1 egg

1 egg white

½ cup (3.75 ounces, 106 grams) firmly packed brown sugar

Toast the almonds in a dry frying pan until they are slightly browned; then chop them finely by hand or grind in a food processor until coarsely ground.

In a large bowl, whisk the egg and the egg white together with the sugar until frothy. Stir in the slightly cooled butter, then add the almonds and stir to a smooth batter.

Roll out the chilled dough to ⅛-inch (.25 centimeter) thickness and press into the pie pan. It is easiest to roll out the dough between two sheets of plastic wrap. Pour the batter into the pan and spread it out evenly with a spatula.

Bake for 20 to 25 minutes. The crust should be golden brown and the batter should be set. Remove from the oven and let cool before serving.

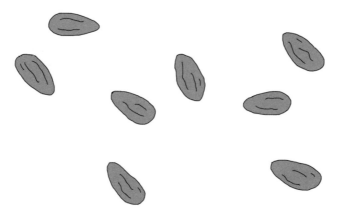

hasselnötskaka med kaffe

HAZELNUT COFFEE CAKE

makes one 9-inch (23-centimeter) cake

This cake actually has nothing to do with what many people know as coffee cake; the name comes from the addition of brewed coffee to the batter, a distinct taste when paired with hazelnuts. This cake is airy enough not to feel heavy, but thick enough that you get the satisfaction of biting into something substantial. As opposed to a lot of fluffy cake recipes, which use baking powder as a leavener, this one depends on the power of egg whites, which makes for the perfect consistency. The same method is used in the Cardamom Cake (page 30) and the Kinuski Caramel Cake (page 88).

Hazelnuts are quite common in Swedish baking; the key in this recipe is toasting them, which helps intensify the flavor.

Preheat the oven to 350°F (175°C). Grease and flour a 9-inch (23-centimeter) springform pan.

In a saucepan, melt the butter. Remove from the heat and set aside to cool.

Toast the hazelnuts in a dry frying pan until they are slightly browned; then grind them in a food processor until almost finely ground.

In a bowl, whisk together the egg yolks and brown sugar until frothy. All the sugar should be dissolved and the batter should have a lighter color. Pour the slightly

10½ tablespoons (5.25 ounces, 148 grams) unsalted butter

½ cup (2.5 ounces, 71 grams) raw hazelnuts

3 egg yolks

¼ cup (1.88 ounces, 53 grams) firmly packed brown sugar

½ cup (2.5 ounces, 71 grams) all-purpose flour

3 tablespoons cold coffee (preferably espresso)

¼ teaspoon salt

3 egg whites, room temperature

¾ cup (5.25 ounces, 148 grams) natural cane sugar

cooled butter into the egg yolk and sugar mixture and whisk together. Sift the flour and stir it carefully into the batter together with the hazelnuts, coffee, and salt. Stir as little as possible until you get a smooth, even batter.

In a separate, grease-free bowl, whisk the egg whites, ideally with an electric mixer. When soft peaks form, add the cane sugar little by little. Mix until the batter forms stiff peaks.

Carefully fold the sugar and egg white mixture into the batter and keep folding until the batter is evenly blended. Be careful not to overstir. Pour the batter directly into the pan.

Bake for 30 to 40 minutes. The cake is done when a toothpick or knife inserted into the center comes out clean. If the cake starts to get a golden brown color earlier (which can happen after 20 minutes), remove it from the oven, cover it with aluminum foil, and put back in the oven. This will prevent the top of the cake from burning.

Remove the cake from the oven and let cool slightly before serving.

kärleksmums
CHOCOLATE COFFEE SQUARES

makes 24 squares

Kärleksmums is one of those bake-at-home recipes that always makes you feel good, no matter what kind of mood you're in. In Swedish, the interjection *mums* means "yummy," and added to *kärlek*, it directly translates to "love yummy." Just like other recipes that have been passed along many times, this one has several names, including *fiffirutor*, *mockarutor*, and *snoddas*.

These cakes are the perfect blend of dark chocolate and strong coffee. Kärleksmums is classically made with a confectioners' sugar frosting, but we think it's nicer with the more luxurious ganache. Save a few tablespoons from your morning cup of coffee so you can add it to the ganache when you bake these later in the afternoon; the perfect thing to enjoy on a cold autumn day.

Preheat the oven to 375°F (190°C). Grease and flour a 9 by 13-inch (23 by 33-centimeter) baking pan.

In a saucepan, melt the butter. Remove from the heat and set aside.

In a large bowl, stir together the flour, cocoa powder, baking powder, and salt.

cake

10 tablespoons (5 ounces, 142 grams) unsalted butter

2 cups (10 ounces, 284 grams) all-purpose flour

4 tablespoons unsweetened cocoa powder

2 teaspoons baking powder

½ teaspoon salt

2 eggs

1 cup (7 ounces, 198 grams) natural cane sugar

¾ cup (180 milliliters) milk

1 teaspoon pure vanilla extract

ganache

½ cup (120 milliliters) heavy cream

3 tablespoons cold coffee

4 ounces (113 grams) 70% bittersweet dark chocolate

2 tablespoons (1 ounce, 28 grams) butter

topping

About ½ cup (1.5 ounces, 42 grams) unsweetened shredded coconut

In a separate bowl, whisk the eggs together with the sugar until frothy. Add the milk, melted butter, and vanilla and whisk until well blended. Sift and fold in the flour mixture and keep folding until you have a smooth and even batter. Pour the batter into the baking pan.

Bake for 12 to 17 minutes. The cake is done when a toothpick or knife inserted into the center comes out clean. Remove from the oven and let cool.

To prepare the ganache, heat the cream and coffee in a saucepan over medium heat until the liquid starts to bubble around the edges. Lower the heat and add the chocolate, stirring constantly until melted. Turn off the heat, add the butter, and stir until melted. Let cool for about 1 hour.

Spread the ganache over the cake and top with shredded coconut. Cut into 24 equally sized squares to serve.

Store in an airtight container in the refrigerator or in the freezer.

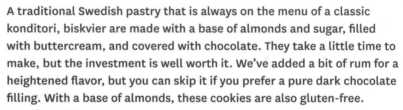

chokladbiskvier

CHOCOLATE BUTTERCREAM ALMOND ROUNDS

makes 20 rounds

A traditional Swedish pastry that is always on the menu of a classic konditori, biskvier are made with a base of almonds and sugar, filled with buttercream, and covered with chocolate. They take a little time to make, but the investment is well worth it. We've added a bit of rum for a heightened flavor, but you can skip it if you prefer a pure dark chocolate filling. With a base of almonds, these cookies are also gluten-free.

If you blanch your own almonds, be sure to pat them dry. If you use store-bought almonds, you may end up with a coarse, dry meal. In this case, a slight splash of water in the mixture may help, but you don't want it too wet. Store the cookies in an airtight container in the refrigerator or freezer.

Preheat the oven to 400°F (200°C). Line a baking sheet with a silicone baking mat or parchment paper.

Mix the almonds, sugar, and almond extract in a food processor until the almonds are finely ground and the mixture starts to stick together.

In a grease-free bowl, whisk the egg white, ideally with an electric mixer, until soft peaks form. Fold the egg white in with the almond mixture and keep folding with a spatula until it forms an almond paste.

rounds

1 cup (5 ounces, 142 grams) blanched almonds

½ cup (3.5 ounces, 99 grams) natural cane sugar

¼ teaspoon pure almond extract

1 egg white, room temperature

filling

2.5 ounces (70 grams)
70% bittersweet dark chocolate

6 tablespoons (3 ounces,
85 grams) unsalted butter,
room temperature

2 tablespoons natural cane sugar

1 egg yolk

2 teaspoons rum, or 4 teaspoons
lemon juice or orange juice

topping

3.5 to 5 ounces (100 to 140 grams)
70% bittersweet dark chocolate
(more makes for easier dipping
and leftover melted chocolate)

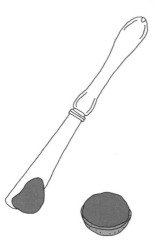

Divide the paste into 20 equal parts. Roll each part into a ball and place it on the baking sheet. Flatten each ball slightly with your hand.

Bake for 12 to 15 minutes, until the cookies are golden brown. Remove from the oven and transfer the cookies from the baking sheet to the counter to cool.

To prepare the filling, melt the chocolate in the top of a double boiler, or in a clean heatproof bowl placed in a saucepan of barely simmering water. Remove from the heat and set aside.

In a separate bowl, cream together the butter, sugar, and egg yolk until the batter is well blended and smooth. Stir in the rum and fold in the melted chocolate until you get a smooth and even batter.

When the cookie rounds are completely cool, spread a bit of the buttercream filling on the flat part of each cookie. Make sure that there is slightly more filling in the middle of the cookie, to form a slight mound. Place the cookies on a plate and then put in the refrigerator or freezer, uncovered, until the filling is stiff, about 15 to 30 minutes.

To prepare the topping, melt the chocolate in the top of a double boiler, or in a clean heatproof bowl placed in a saucepan of barely simmering water. Carefully dip each cookie into the chocolate so that the butter-cream filling is covered and set aside on the counter or on a plate until the topping hardens.

kokostoppar

COCONUT PEAKS

makes 25 to 30 cookies

Kokostoppar are the Swedish version of a classic coconut macaroon and most certainly a staple on the fika cookie platter. This is a recipe that works well with many variations. For a twist, try adding a teaspoon of freshly grated ginger or dipping the tips in dark chocolate. These are also gluten-free.

Preheat the oven to 350°F (175°C). Grease a baking sheet or line it with parchment paper or a silicone baking mat

In a saucepan, melt the butter. Remove from the heat and set aside.

In a bowl, lightly whisk together the eggs and sugar. Fold in the coconut and salt and the slightly cooled butter. Let the batter sit for about 15 minutes.

Scoop tablespoon-size portions of the batter onto the baking sheet and shape them into peaked mounds.

Bake for 10 to 12 minutes, until the cookies are a light golden brown. Remove from the oven and let cool.

Store in an airtight container.

3½ tablespoons (1.75 ounces, 50 grams) unsalted butter

2 eggs

⅔ cup (4.67 ounces, 132 grams) natural cane sugar

2¼ cups (6.75 ounces, 191 grams) unsweetened shredded coconut

¼ teaspoon salt

chokladbollar

CHOCOLATE BALLS

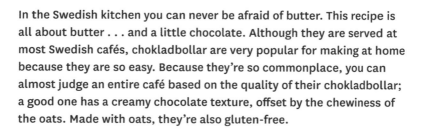

makes 20 to 25 balls

In the Swedish kitchen you can never be afraid of butter. This recipe is all about butter . . . and a little chocolate. Although they are served at most Swedish cafés, chokladbollar are very popular for making at home because they are so easy. Because they're so commonplace, you can almost judge an entire café based on the quality of their chokladbollar; a good one has a creamy chocolate texture, offset by the chewiness of the oats. Made with oats, they're also gluten-free.

2 cups (7 ounces, 198 grams) rolled oats

½ cup (4 ounces, 113 grams) unsalted butter, room temperature

¼ cup (1.75 ounces, 50 grams) natural cane sugar

¼ cup (.75 ounce, 21 grams) unsweetened cocoa powder

1 teaspoon pure vanilla extract

½ teaspoon salt

About ½ cup (1.5 ounces, 42 grams) shredded coconut

In a food processor, pulse the oats into a coarse meal. You want just a little bit of texture, so don't grind them all the way. If you don't have a food processor, use the smallest oats you can find, as they are better for the final texture of the chocolate balls.

In a bowl, cream together the butter and sugar. Add the cocoa powder and vanilla and cream together until well blended; then add the oats and the salt. Using your hands, mix all of the ingredients together.

Roll the mixture into small balls, about a tablespoon for each one. Roll each ball in the shredded coconut until fully coated.

Store in an airtight container in the refrigerator, or in the freezer for longer periods.

kladdkaka

STICKY CHOCOLATE CAKE

makes one 9-inch (23-centimeter) cake

The direct translation for "kladdkaka" is "sticky cake." You don't need much more of a descriptor than that. Kladdkaka is one of the basics of Swedish home baking, the kind of recipe that you memorize and can make at the drop of a hat. In college it serves to fuel all-nighters; on a birthday or other special occasion, you might serve it with a dollop of fresh whipped cream. A variation on the classic recipe, this one uses ground almonds instead of flour, giving it a chewier texture than the original version, and perfect for serving to gluten-free friends.

Preheat the oven to 350°F (175°C). Grease a 9-inch (23-centimeter) springform pan or round baking dish.

Grind the almonds in a food processor until almost finely ground.

In a saucepan, melt the butter. Remove from the heat and set aside to cool.

In a bowl, whisk together the eggs and sugar. Sift in the cocoa powder, add the salt, and stir together. Add the almonds, followed by the slightly cooled butter; stir until you get a smooth batter.

½ cup (2.5 ounces, 71 grams) blanched almonds

½ cup (4 ounces, 113 grams) unsalted butter

2 eggs

1 cup (7 ounces, 198 grams) natural cane sugar

⅓ cup (1 ounce, 28 grams) plus 1 tablespoon unsweetened cocoa powder

¼ teaspoon salt

3 to 4 teaspoons poppy seeds (optional)

Pour the batter into the pan. Sprinkle the poppy seeds evenly on top.

Bake for 15 to 20 minutes. The cake is done when it is set on top but still sticky on the inside. You can check this by carefully lifting one side of the cake pan; if the cake still appears runny, it needs to bake longer; if it doesn't move, it's done.

Let the cake cool before serving.

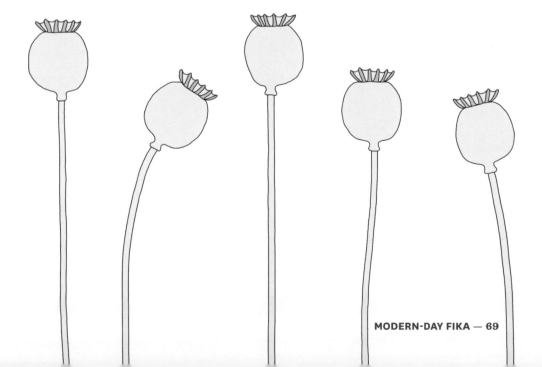

hastbullar

QUICK BUNS

makes 12 to 15 buns

While nowadays we often like to use long and complicated names for dishes, the titles of many classic Swedish baked goods are incredibly simple; a short and sweet name that tells you everything. Such is the case with hastbullar. Bullar, which means "bun," is a common fika offering, albeit in many different forms and flavors. But while other bullar recipes are a little more involved (like Vetebullar, page 26), this one is made for the person who just invited some friends over for fika and doesn't have a whole lot of time to prepare. *Hast* in Swedish means "hurry" or "haste"; in other words, the kind of thing you can whip up when you're pressed for time. The original version is fairly simple, but this one adds dried figs and toasted hazelnuts for a little twist.

dough

2 cups (10 ounces, 284 grams) all-purpose flour

2 teaspoons whole cardamom seeds, crushed

2 teaspoons baking powder

¼ cup (1.75 ounces, 50 grams) natural cane sugar

7 tablespoons (3.5 ounces, 99 grams) unsalted butter

½ cup dried figs (2.62 ounces, 75 grams), finely chopped

1 egg

¾ cup (180 milliliters) milk

topping

1 egg, beaten

¼ cup (1.25 ounces, 35 grams) toasted hazelnuts, chopped, or pearl sugar

Preheat the oven to 425°F (220°C). Line a muffin pan with paper liners or place paper liners on a baking sheet. These buns hold their form without paper liners, but using them makes for a nicer-looking presentation. If you don't use paper liners, be sure to grease the baking sheet, or line with parchment paper or a silicone baking mat.

In a large bowl, mix together the flour, crushed cardamom, baking powder, and sugar. Using your hands, add the butter in small pieces and work together with your fingertips until the dough resembles a coarse meal. Add the figs to the mixture, stirring together until evenly mixed in.

In a small bowl, whisk together 1 of the eggs and the milk. Stir into the flour mixture until you get a sticky, well-blended batter. Drop a large spoonful of the batter into each paper liner.

Brush the beaten on top of each bun. Sprinkle with hazelnuts.

Bake for 10 to 15 minutes, until the tops of the buns are golden brown. Remove from the oven and let cool.

Eat fresh or store in an airtight container in the freezer.

kronans kaka

ALMOND POTATO CAKE

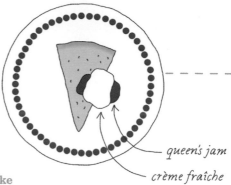

queen's jam

crème fraîche

makes one 9-inch (23-centimeter) cake

Originating in the late 1800s, *kronans kaka* is made with mashed potatoes as a replacement for flour, which in the hard times of that particular era was used sparingly. It was also an excellent way to put extra cooked potatoes, a staple of the Swedish diet, to good use. While nowadays few of us have to ration our flour, it is refreshing to have a dessert that's made without it, and it's perfect for serving to gluten-free friends.

You can eat this on its own, but it pairs well with fresh fruit and a dollop of whipped cream, or even crème fraîche, and a little bit of Queen's Jam (page 91) or Rhubarb Compote (page 80). You can also use toasted or blanched almonds, instead of raw, for a slightly different taste.

Preheat the oven to 350°F (175°C). Grease and flour a 9-inch (23-centimeter) round baking pan.

Cream together the butter and sugar. Mix in one egg at a time, stirring until you get a creamy consistency. Add the almonds and lemon zest and stir until smooth.

Mash the potatoes using a fork or a pastry blender, until you have a smooth consistency with no large pieces left. Add to the batter and stir together until well blended.

7 tablespoons (3.5 ounces, 99 grams) unsalted butter, room temperature

½ cup (3.5 ounces, 99 grams) natural cane sugar

2 eggs

1 cup (5 ounces, 142 grams) raw almonds, finely ground

Zest of 1 small lemon (1 to 2 tablespoons)

2 boiled, medium-size (about 7 ounces, 200 grams) potatoes

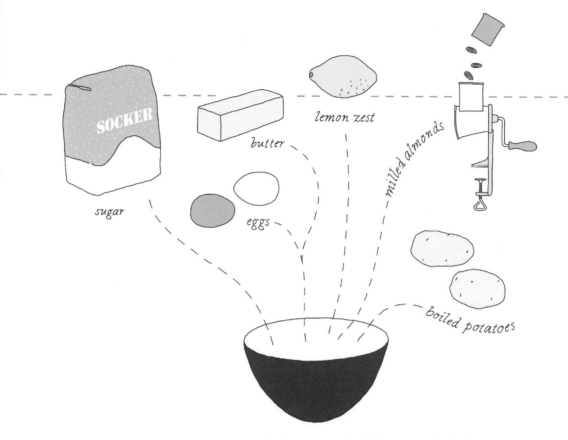

SOCKER

sugar

butter

eggs

lemon zest

milled almonds

boiled potatoes

Pour the batter into the baking pan and bake for 40 to 50 minutes, until the top is golden brown. If the cake starts to get a golden brown color earlier (which can happen after 30 minutes), remove it from the oven, cover it with aluminum foil, and put back in the oven. This will prevent the top of the cake from burning.

Let cool, then cut into slices and serve directly from the pan.

CHAPTER 3

- - - - - - -

the outdoor
season

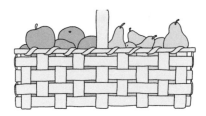

the days are long and the nights are short. The warm, gentle air carries smells of saltwater, wildflowers, and freshly picked berries. Food is eaten outside whenever possible and days are spent barefoot. This is Swedish summer.

Summer is a holy time in Sweden, kicked off by the celebration of *midsommar*, the summer solstice. Through the months of July and August, people escape to their summer homes, crossing their fingers for a season of plentiful sun and limited raindrops. After a long winter, summer is a time when the Swedish spirit flourishes; the traditionally reserved people of the North let go a little; gardens are opened for evening parties; and the coffee at fika flows freely.

As most Swedes have at least a month off during the summer, this is a season that comes with an expectation of relaxing; lazy mornings in bed reading the paper while the sun peeks through the curtains, afternoons walking in the forest on the hunt for wild berries. Swedes have an affinity for the natural world, and when the sun shines they spend as much time outside as possible.

Summer vacations almost always involve a few days of berry picking. Some are lucky enough to have a gooseberry or black currant bush in their backyard, but even for those who don't, finding a *självplock*, "pick-your-own," strawberry field or a forest of wild blueberries is never hard. You return home with fingers stained with the blues and reds of fresh fruit and reused plastic containers or buckets filled with ample amounts of the season's bounty, waiting to be turned into a culinary delight—if you can manage to save more than you eat right off the bush.

Soon comes the transition to fall, a season that Swedes love as much as summer. Although the temperature cools down, the sun still shines, and sweaters and boots are donned in preparation for forest excursions to go mushroom picking. Apples straight from the tree make their way into cakes, and Swedes begin the preparation for the colder season ahead.

sylta och safta — MAKING JAM AND CORDIALS

Berries, fruits, and even flowers are used in jams, cordials, and baked goods, making berry-flavored anything indicative of the season. Much like in other European countries, there is a tradition of homemade jam, storing up the flavors of summer for use during the dark days of winter.

Beyond jam, the other common use for freshly picked berries is turning them into *saft*, a classic Swedish drink. While the Swedish cordial, a fruity concentrate that's mixed with water before being served, is found in abundance in grocery stores, there's no better kind than homemade.

Berries are boiled down into the thick, sugary concentrate that's the fika libation of choice for children. No summer picnic is complete without it.

fika outside . . . and in

Summer is all about making time for fika outside. A round of cinnamon buns served with a pitcher of rhubarb cordial pairs well with a warm afternoon. In rural Sweden, farmhouses open up seasonal fika spots, cozy garden spaces that serve fresh breads, strong coffee, and a homemade baked good or two. Families spend afternoons at the ocean or the lake, with parents laying down picnic blankets and pulling out full fika spreads while children play in the water. Friends in the city get together at outdoor seating areas; any café that doesn't have a good patio simply isn't worth going to. The sun and warm breeze are made for enjoyment.

But even in the summer, rainy days abound, and just like in the fall and winter, fika provides a time to cozy up with a warm drink while the summer drops stream down the window. Throw a picnic blanket on the floor, put out a few slices of Fyriskaka (page 94), and you'll find that the gray lull of summer rain is almost enjoyable. As autumn rolls around, pack a thermos and an extra sweater and head out to harvest your own apples.

Swedes aren't picky; living in a temperate climate means that they are just as happy sitting outside in a wool sweater and a scarf as they are basking in the sun-kissed days of summer. But the point is to be outdoors; when there's sun, no matter what the temperature, it's meant to be enjoyed. Summer and fall are cherished periods not only because there is plenty of time for adventures, but also because there's food to go with it, from the rhubarb stalks of early summer to the apples of autumn.

recipes

Summer is for celebrating; it's a time for being indulgent. Sleep in, stay up late, and eat as much rhubarb as humanly possible. Then comes autumn and the apple harvest and the chance to forage for mushrooms. These recipes are inspired by warm days and walking in the countryside harvesting berries or picking fruit in the garden. If you don't have access to picking berries or fruit yourself, head over to a farmers' market and buy a little more than you usually would. You're going to want the extra bounty.

rabarberkompott

RHUBARB COMPOTE

makes one 16-ounce (473-milliliter) jar

Be they stalks from your garden or from the farmers' market, fresh rhubarb is always the promise of good things. One of the easiest ways to prepare rhubarb is to turn it into a compote, which afterward can be used for a variety of fika-friendly dishes. In fact, as a compote, rhubarb can be good for dessert or even a meal. Add it to your morning yogurt or oatmeal for an extra kick, or spoon it up in Mandelmusslor (Almond Tartlet Shells, page 124) with a little whipped cream for a simple summer dessert. This compote is slightly sour, as the Swedes like it; if you want it sweeter, add a bit more sugar.

Rinse the rhubarb stalks and peel off the skin using a small knife; then chop the stalks into small pieces and place in a saucepan with the mint. Pour the sugar on top.

On medium-high heat, bring everything to a boil, while occasionally stirring. The mixture will look dry in the beginning, but the rhubarb will quickly juice up, so there is no need to add any water. Skim off and discard any foam that appears on the surface. Let the compote cook on medium heat, stirring occasionally, until all of the rhubarb pieces have

10 to 12 (2 pounds, almost 1 kilogram) rhubarb stalks

3 small sprigs mint

1¼ cups (8.75 ounces, 248 grams) natural cane sugar

broken down and the sugar has completely dissolved. Remove from the heat.

Run the compote in a blender until smooth, then pour it back into the saucepan and let it cook for a few more minutes before pouring into a clean sterilized jar. Turn the jar upside down to create a vacuum. Let cool completely.

Store in the refrigerator and eat within a week. If you want to store it longer, place the compote in the freezer.

rabarbersaft

RHUBARB CORDIAL

makes about two 25-ounce (750-milliliter) bottles

Besides compote, another easy way to put rhubarb to use is in saft, cordial, a wonderful option for summer fika when you want something different from a cup of coffee. Pour a pitcher of *rabarbersaft* and serve with a tray of Vetebullar (page 26) in the garden, and you have the ideal summer afternoon break. This cordial is also delicious as a summer cocktail, with the addition of lime, mint, gin, and tonic water.

Wash the rhubarb stalks and cut them into small pieces; there is no need to remove the skin. Place together with the water in a large saucepan. Bring the water to a boil and let simmer until the rhubarb pieces fall apart. Skim off and discard any foam that appears on the surface.

Remove from the heat and strain the liquid through a clean kitchen towel or cheesecloth. Return the strained rhubarb juice to the saucepan; stir in the sugar, cloves, and cinnamon stick and bring to a boil. When the sugar has dissolved completely, remove the cordial from the heat. Remove the cloves and cinnamon stick and pour into clean sterilized bottles. Pour the liquid all the way up to the top and seal the bottle immediately.

10 to 12 (2 pounds, almost 1 kilogram) rhubarb stalks

6⅓ cups (1½ liters) water

2½ cups (1⅛ pounds, 496 grams) natural cane sugar

5 whole cloves

1 cinnamon stick

Store the bottles in the refrigerator and consume within 6 weeks. If you want to keep it longer, freeze the cordial in a plastic container and scoop out portions as needed.

When you're ready to serve the cordial, dilute it with tap or sparkling water, using 1 part cordial to 4 parts water.

flädersaft

ELDERFLOWER CORDIAL

makes three to four 25-ounce (750-milliliter) bottles

If there is a cordial that tastes like Sweden, *flädersaft* is it. A traditional summer drink, it is readily available in Swedish stores and markets, but the homemade version is always the best. Elderflower can be found in gardens but most often grows in the wild, and most Swedes know of a few bushes they can trek to in the forest to retrieve the blossoms. Outside of Sweden, you have to grow your own or forage for it, making your fika taste just a little more special. This recipe is one Johanna learned from a gardener named Göran.

Separate the tiny flowers from the stalk using a fork or a pair of scissors. Rinse the lemons in hot water and slice them thinly. Place the flowers in a clean bucket together with the lemon slices.

In a saucepan, bring the water to a boil and stir in the sugar. When the sugar has completely dissolved, stir in the citric acid.

Remove the sugar mixture from the heat and pour over the flowers and lemon slices. Let stand, covered, for 3 to 4 days in a cool place. You want to be sure that the flowers and lemons are completely submerged; if necessary, place a plate on top to push them down.

40 elderflower clusters

4 lemons

8½ cups (2 liters) water

10 cups (4⅜ pounds, 2 kilograms) natural cane sugar

2 teaspoons (1 ounce, 30 grams) citric acid

Strain the liquid to remove the flowers and pour into clean sterilized glass bottles. Store the bottles in the refrigerator and consume within 6 weeks. If you want to keep it longer, freeze the cordial in a plastic container and scoop out portions as needed.

When you're ready to serve the cordial, dilute it with tap or sparkling water, using 1 part cordial to 4 parts water.

hallonpaj med vaniljsås

RASPBERRY PIE WITH VANILLA SAUCE

makes one 10-inch (25.5-centimeter) pie

A bucket of freshly picked raspberries is like a pot of gold, and this pie makes good use of them. A friend of Johanna's mother, Mona, who used to make the pie with applesauce, inspired this recipe. We think it's best with raspberries, though, and we've topped it off with this classic vanilla sauce, which is often used on Swedish fruit pies.

In a bowl, cream together the butter and sugar. Add the egg and vanilla and work together until well blended.

In a separate bowl, mix together the flour and baking powder; then add it to the butter mixture. Work together with your hands until you can make the dough into a ball. Shape the dough into a long roll, as this makes it easier to roll out when the dough has chilled. Place in the refrigerator for at least 30 minutes.

Preheat the oven to 350°F (175°C). Grease a 10-inch (25.5-centimeter) springform pan.

With a rolling pin, roll out two-thirds of the dough to a 10-inch (25.5-centimeter) round, slightly thicker than ⅛ inch (.25 centimeter). It is easiest to roll out the dough between 2 sheets of plastic wrap. Place the rolled-out dough in the pan. Arrange the berries on top and sprinkle them with the brown sugar.

dough

9 tablespoons (4.5 ounces, 128 grams) unsalted butter, room temperature

½ cup (3.5 ounces, 99 grams) natural cane sugar

1 egg

¼ teaspoon pure vanilla extract

1¾ cups (8.75 ounces, 248 grams) all-purpose flour

1½ teaspoons baking powder

filling

About 4 cups (about 18 ounces, 510 grams) fresh raspberries

2 tablespoons brown sugar

vaniljsås (classic vanilla sauce)

1 large vanilla bean

1 cup (240 milliliters) half-and-half

1 cup (240 milliliters) heavy cream

3 egg yolks

⅓ cup (2.33 ounces, 66 grams) natural cane sugar

Roll out the rest of the dough to the same thickness. Using a pastry cutter or knife, cut the dough into ⅜-inch- (1-centimeter) wide strips. Crisscross the strips diagonally over the berries, creating a lattice top.

Bake for 30 to 40 minutes. The pie is done when you can see juice from the fruit lightly bubbling. If the pie starts to get a golden brown color earlier (which can happen after 15 minutes), remove it from the oven, cover it with aluminum foil, and put back in the oven.

Remove the pie from the oven and let cool.

To make the vanilla sauce, cut the vanilla bean in half lengthwise. Place in a saucepan together with the half-and-half and cream. Bring to a boil. Remove from the heat and let cool for about 15 minutes.

Whisk together the egg yolks and sugar until frothy. Pour over the cooled vanilla mixture. Return to the heat and simmer very carefully at medium to low heat, making sure not to let it boil. Whisk constantly until the sauce begins to thicken, about 2 minutes. Cooking longer will make it more of a custard than a sauce. Remove the vanilla bean and let cool in the refrigerator.

Serve the pie with the vanilla sauce, either poured over or served on the side. The sauce will keep in the refrigerator for 1 to 2 days but is best served the day that it is prepared.

kinuskikaka

KINUSKI CARAMEL CAKE

makes one 9-inch (23-centimeter) cake

Originating from Finland, *kinuskikakku* (or *kinuskikaka* in Swedish) is a cake topped with a thick caramel, called *kinuski* in Finnish. This recipe comes from the Åströms, Johanna's Finnish side of the family. It's sweet and decadent and not for the lighthearted. To offset the sweetness, we've added a layer of lingonberries, a Swedish foraging favorite. The tart flavor of the berries combines with the caramel for a unique and delicious cake. If you can't get lingonberries, red currants or raspberries will do the trick.

Preheat the oven to 350°F (175°C). Grease and flour a 9-inch (23-centimeter) springform pan.

In a saucepan, melt the butter. Remove from the heat and set aside to cool.

Grind the almonds in a food processor until almost finely ground.

In a bowl, whisk together the egg yolks and brown sugar until frothy; all the sugar should be dissolved and the batter should have a lighter color. Pour the butter into the egg yolk and sugar mixture and whisk together a little longer. Sift the flour and stir it carefully into the batter together with the almonds,

cake

10½ tablespoons (5.25 ounces, 148 grams) unsalted butter

1 cup (5 ounces, 142 grams) blanched almonds

3 egg yolks, room temperature

¼ cup (1.88 ounces, 53 grams) firmly packed brown sugar

½ cup (2.5 ounces, 71 grams) all-purpose flour

¼ teaspoon pure almond extract

¼ teaspoon salt

3 egg whites, room temperature

¾ cup (5.25 ounces, 148 grams) natural cane sugar

kinuski

1 cup (240 milliliters) heavy cream

1 cup (7.5 ounces, 213 grams) firmly packed brown sugar

topping

1 handful lingonberries

almond extract, and salt. Stir as little as possible to get a smooth, even batter.

In a separate, grease-free bowl, whisk the egg whites, ideally with an electric mixer. When soft peaks form, add the cane sugar little by little. Whisk until stiff peaks form. Carefully fold the sugar and egg white mixture into the batter and keep folding until the batter is evenly blended. Be careful not to overstir. Pour directly into the baking pan.

Bake for 30 to 40 minutes. The cake is done when a toothpick or knife inserted into the center comes out clean. If the cake starts to get a golden brown color earlier (which can happen after 20 minutes), remove it from the oven, cover it with aluminum foil, and put back in the oven.

Remove the cake from the oven and let cool. Once cool, remove the cake from the pan.

To prepare the kinuski, in a saucepan, bring the cream and sugar to a boil; then cook on medium heat, stirring occasionally. Cook for 30 to 40 minutes, until thick. To test if the kinuski is done, insert a spoon into the sauce and remove. Raise it above the saucepan for a few minutes to let it cool off a bit. The kinuski should have a thick consistency and stick to the spoon, similar to caramel.

CONTINUED

Remove the kinuski from the heat and let cool slightly.
While it is still a little warm, and therefore runny,
pour the kinuski little by little onto the cake. As it gets
poured on, it will set and harden a little, so you can
keep pouring without the risk of pouring it every-
where. Let cool completely.

Arrange the lingonberries on top of the cake. Then
slice and serve.

If you don't want to use all of the kinuski on the cake,
you can store the extra in a glass jar. It's great as a
topping for ice cream or spread on cookies.

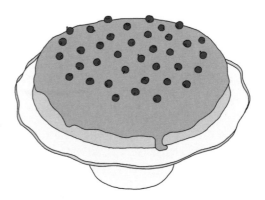

drottningsylt

QUEEN'S JAM

makes one 16-ounce (473-milliliter) jar

Half blueberries and half raspberries, *drottningsylt* is a staple in the category of Swedish preserves. It has a rich color and taste that make it ideal for Jam Thumbprint Cookies (page 40) and also as a sweet spread on any of the breads and crackers in chapter 5 of this book. If you can't get fresh berries, you can make the jam with frozen ones, but note that the weight measurements for the berries are based on fresh ones.

2 cups (about 9 ounces, 255 grams) fresh raspberries

1 cup (about 5 ounces, 141 grams) fresh blueberries

¾ cup (5.25 ounces, 148 grams) natural cane sugar

Place the raspberries, blueberries, and sugar in a medium-size saucepan. Bring to a boil and cook over medium heat until it reaches the desired thickness, 15 to 30 minutes depending on the juiciness of the fruit. (To test the consistency, place a small plate in the freezer. Once the plate is cold, remove it from the freezer and drop a spoonful of jam onto it. Let it sit for a few minutes, then push the jam with your finger. If it has gelled and the skin wrinkles, then it is set. If it's still liquid, continue cooking until you reach the consistency you want.)

Remove from the heat and pour the jam into a clean sterilized jar. Screw on the lid and turn the jar upside down to create a vacuum. Let cool completely. Store in the refrigerator and eat within a month. If you want to store it longer, place the jam in the freezer.

mandelkaka med björnbär

BLACKBERRY ALMOND CAKE

makes one 9-inch (23-centimeter) cake

When it's summer, you don't always want to spend a lot of time in a warm kitchen baking. Therefore, it's good to know a simple cake recipe that can be put together in minutes and that you can change depending on which berries you have on hand. This is exactly that recipe, which comes from Anna's Aunt Lotta. While the cake is delicious with blackberries, you can also use it as a base for other berries and fruits: raspberries, blueberries, and even halved plums work well. Serve the cake by itself or with freshly whipped cream. This cake is also good with a dusting of cinnamon and sugar on top.

Preheat the oven to 400°F (200°C). Grease and flour a 9-inch (23-centimeter) round baking pan.

In a small saucepan, melt the butter. Remove from the heat and set aside to cool.

In a large bowl, whisk together the eggs, sugar, and almond extract until frothy. Pour in the slightly cooled butter and stir until well blended. Sift in the flour and mix until the batter is smooth and creamy.

Pour the batter into the baking pan. Scatter the blackberries evenly over the top. You don't need to

6 tablespoons (3 ounces, 85 grams) unsalted butter

2 eggs

¾ cup (5.25 ounces, 148 grams) natural cane sugar

1 teaspoon pure almond extract

1 cup (5 ounces, 142 grams) all-purpose flour

About 1 cup (4 to 5 ounces, 113 to 142 grams) fresh blackberries

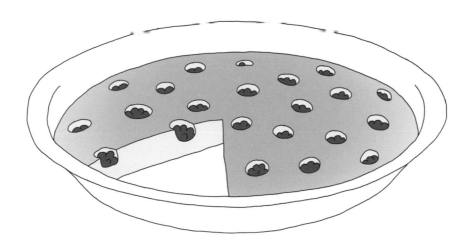

press the berries into the cake; their weight makes them sink a bit during baking.

Bake for 20 to 30 minutes, until golden brown on top. The cake is done when a toothpick or knife inserted into the center comes out clean. Remove the cake and let cool before serving.

fyriskaka

CLASSIC APPLE CAKE

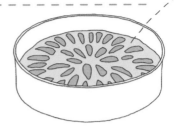

makes one 9-inch (23-centimeter) cake

When late summer turns into early fall, fyriskaka is the perfect fika treat. A moist apple and cinnamon cake, this recipe is a true Swedish classic. Like many other variations of this cake, this version has a little crushed cardamom added for extra taste. You can serve the cake on its own, but it's also amazing with whipped cream or even a little vanilla ice cream.

Preheat the oven to 350°F (175°C). Grease and flour a 9-inch (23-centimeter) springform pan.

In a small saucepan, melt the butter. Remove from the heat and add the cardamom, then set aside to cool.

Peel the apples and slice them thinly.

In a large bowl, mix together 2 tablespoons of the brown sugar with the cinnamon; then add the apples and carefully turn them so that they are evenly coated. Set aside.

In another large bowl, whisk together the slightly cooled butter and cane sugar. Add the eggs one by one, whisking until evenly blended. Sift in the flour and baking powder and stir together carefully until you get a smooth batter.

9 tablespoons (4.5 ounces, 128 grams) unsalted butter

1 teaspoon whole cardamom seeds, crushed

3 to 4 medium-size apples (about 1 pound, 454 grams)

3 to 4 tablespoons brown sugar

1½ teaspoons cinnamon

⅔ cup (4.67 ounces, 132 grams) natural cane sugar

2 eggs

1 cup (5 ounces, 142 grams) all-purpose flour

½ teaspoon baking powder

cinnamon

apple

brown sugar

Spread the batter in the baking pan. Place the apple slices on top of the batter in a circular formation; the pieces should be close together. Sprinkle the remaining 1 to 2 tablespoons brown sugar on top. If you like, you can sprinkle with a little cardamom as well.

Bake for 30 to 40 minutes. The cake is done when a toothpick or knife inserted into the center comes out clean. Remove from oven and let cool before serving.

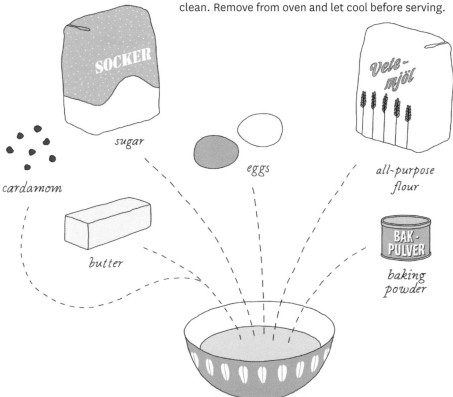

SOCKER

sugar

cardamom

butter

eggs

vete-mjöl

all-purpose flour

BAK-PULVER

baking powder

CHAPTER 4

----

celebrating more than the everyday

ust as fika is an excuse to take a moment to celebrate the everyday, it's also a crucial part of actual celebrations, from birthdays to Christmas. Dressed up with a few special baked goods, fika can be a party.

namsdagar — NAME DAYS

The custom of *namsdagar* originates from the Christian calendar of saints. Every saint had his or her own feast day, and those named after a certain saint also celebrate on that day. Nowadays, the Swedish calendar has been adapted to incorporate many more modern names that don't necessarily have saintly roots, but the celebration part of the tradition still holds, and a name day is almost like an extra birthday (without the stress and anxiety of turning yet another year older!). You might get a *grattis på namsdagen,* or "happy name day," card from your grandmother, or a call from your parents, or an invitation to afternoon fika from a friend. Because it's celebratory, a good name day fika goes above and beyond the classic kanelbullar. You're celebrating, after all, so this is a day for tortes and cakes like *prinsesstårta* (see below).

PRINSESSTÅRTA

The Swedish prinsesstårta (princess cake) is indicative of celebration, be it a birthday, a name day, or any other special event. It's a delicious sponge cake, layered with whipped cream and raspberry jam, then covered in green marzipan. Often there is a marzipan rose on top. It's not the easiest of cakes to make at home (although in Sweden you can buy the green marzipan in the baking section of grocery stores and assemble the cake at home), so it's very common to buy a slice from the local konditori. Buying a slice of prinsesstårta, or even a whole cake, boxed up and wrapped in a ribbon, is a sign that you're about to celebrate; and when someone brings the box to you, you know it's a special day.

fettisdagen — FAT TUESDAY

No one can resist Swedish bakery windows in the late winter and early spring. This is the time of the *semla*, a glorious combination of a sweet flour bun, almond paste, and whipped cream. Traditionally made for Fettisdagen, Fat Tuesday, semlor can nowadays be found in Swedish cafés and bakeries all through the early months of the year, from the beginning of the New Year through the end of March.

midsommar — MIDSUMMER

In a country that is dark and cold for much of the year, it should come as no surprise that the Swedes like to celebrate the sun. As such, the tradition of midsommar, celebrating the summer solstice, is as important to Swedes as Christmas and Easter. At midsommar, the longest day of the year, it barely gets dark, and in the north of Sweden, the sun doesn't even set. This leaves room for an all-day and all-night party. Many towns and communities host a day full of events, including dancing around the *midsommarstång*, similar to a maypole, to traditional Swedish songs.

Then comes the food. Most Swedes host or attend some sort of a dinner party, held around a long table outside, even if it's chilly. Pickled herring and new potatoes are served in abundance, and the aquavit and beer flow freely.

Then comes the dessert, an assortment of the best that the season has to offer. The cakes and cookies take a festive form, much like at Christmas, and the treats that you find on the table aren't those of the everyday. The first and foremost midsommar dessert dish is strawberries served with a bowl of whipped cream. Those who have time may bake a *jordgubbstårta* (strawberry cake), layering a sponge cake with the whipped cream and strawberries. But if you aren't in the mood to serve a cake, we recommend a batch of Ginger Meringues (page 106) with strawberries and a little whipped cream. You'll also want to have a round of strong coffee to get you through the nightlong affair.

födelsedag — BIRTHDAY

A classic Swedish birthday party, called *kalas*, almost always involves some sort of tårta, be it a prinsesstårta or other beautiful torte layered with whipped cream. If you're lucky, there will be an assortment of cookies and candies as well. Swedish birthday cakes and tortes always feature whipped cream in lieu of the sugary frosting popular in other parts of the world. Even when the party is too big and there's no time to make a cake, whipped cream still manages to make its way into the picture, in the form of *marängsviss*, meringues topped off with whipped cream and chocolate sauce to make the ultimate Swedish sundae.

jul — CHRISTMAS SEASON

In the midst of a cold and dark winter, December is a monthlong excuse to warm up with good food and drink. Christmas celebrations and preparation happen throughout December, and there are plenty of moments to celebrate. Just as the seven kinds of cookies are essential to an official cookie platter, *julbak* (Christmas baking) is a must during December. Even

Swedes who rarely get out the mixing bowls try their hand at a *pepparkaka* or two this time of year. The smell of spices is indicative of the season, and as you sit in a warm kitchen in front of a plate of Christmas cookies with an Advent candelabrum in the window, you simply wouldn't want to be elsewhere.

advent and lucia

Leading up to Christmas, Swedes celebrate the four Sundays of Advent, lighting an additional candle in the Advent candelabrum every weekend and serving up a tray of goodies. The fika of the season is called *adventskaffe* (Advent coffee), which is a gathering of friends and family every Sunday during December. In the late afternoon you come together to enjoy some *julbakelser* (Christmas baked goods) and a mug of *glögg* (mulled wine), or coffee. You can't say no to a tradition that has you eating goodies all through the month of December, and hosting an adventskaffe is a sure sign that you are embracing Swedish tradition. Common offerings are saffron buns and pepparkakor (page 118), a glorious blend of colors when they are laid out next to each other—the yellow saffron buns pairing well with the dark brown of the spice-filled gingersnaps. Also known as *lussekatter* (page 113), saffron buns are the signature baked good of December 13, the day for the St. Lucia celebration. In many ways, this is the kickoff to the Christmas season, and the julbakelser come in a steady stream from here to Christmas Day.

The drink of choice for the month of December? Coffee is always an excellent pairing, but since you're celebrating the season, you might as well go for glögg (page 126), the Swedish mulled wine that's served this time of year. It's warm and spicy and makes your house smell just like December should. Not in the mood to host a party? Pour yourself a cup of coffee, put a lussekatt on a wooden tray, light a candle, and curl up on the couch. December is meant for feeling cozy.

julafton — CHRISTMAS EVE

Along with the traditional *julbord* (Christmas table) spread of pickled herring, ham, potatoes, and many other seasonal delights, Christmas Eve has plenty of room for baked goods. A cup of glögg may be served with a slice of Saffron Cake with Almond Paste (page 116), and for dessert, delicate Almond Tartlet Shells (page 124) are topped off with berry jam and whipped cream. With so many tasty concoctions available, don't feel bad about eating them all day long, or even kicking the day off with a festive cookie-and-glögg-fueled breakfast.

recipes

Whether you are looking to throw a traditional adventskaffe or make someone feel special on their birthday, these are some of the most essential celebratory recipes that accompany fika for such occasions.

marängtårta med hasselnötter

HAZELNUT MERINGUE TORTE

makes one 9-inch (23-centimeter) torte

For celebrating birthdays, there is nothing more Swedish than whipped cream. Combined with chocolate, hazelnuts, and meringue in this recipe, it makes for a decadent dessert worthy of anyone's special day. This recipe has been a family favorite that Anna's mother, Britta, found in a magazine in the 1970s. For a twist on this torte, add a layer of blackberries, raspberries, or applesauce in the middle.

Preheat the oven to 300°F (150°C). Grease and flour two 9-inch (23-centimeter) round baking pans (springform pans work best). You can also bake this in a single rectangular pan and cut in half to make the individual layers.

To prepare the torte, cream together the butter and sugar. In a separate bowl, whisk the egg yolks and stir into the butter and sugar mixture along with the vanilla and milk. Mix in the flour and baking powder and stir with a spatula until the batter is smooth.

Divide the batter equally between the 2 pans and spread out thinly so that the batter reaches the edges. Sprinkle the chocolate chips evenly over both torte layers, then repeat with the ¾ cup hazelnuts.

torte

6 tablespoons (3 ounces, 85 grams) unsalted butter, room temperature

¾ cup (5.25 ounces, 148 grams) natural cane sugar

4 egg yolks

1 teaspoon pure vanilla extract

¼ cup (60 milliliters) plus 1 tablespoon milk

¾ cup (3.75 ounces, 106 grams) all-purpose flour

1½ teaspoons baking powder

⅓ cup (2 ounces, 57 grams) dark chocolate chips

¾ cup (3.75 ounces, 106 grams) hazelnuts, toasted and finely chopped, plus more for topping

meringue

4 egg whites, room temperature

½ cup (3.5 ounces, 99 grams) natural cane sugar

to finish

1 to 1½ cups (240 to 360 milliliters) heavy whipping cream, whipped, depending on how much you want to cover the torte with

1 to 2 tablespoons unsweetened cocoa powder, for dusting

To prepare the meringue, beat the egg whites with an electric mixer in a large, grease-free bowl until soft peaks form. Add sugar little by little and whisk until stiff peaks form.

Divide the meringue equally between the 2 pans and spread so as to completely cover the chocolate chips and hazelnuts.

Bake for 40 minutes, until the meringue is a deep golden brown and looks crispy. Remove from the oven and let cool in the pans.

Once cool, carefully remove the torte layers.

Place one layer on a serving platter and spread with whipped cream. Place the second layer on top and cover with whipped cream. If you use 1 cup (240 milliliters) of whipping cream, you will have enough to spread between the layers and on top. If you use 1½ cups (360 milliliters), you can cover the sides as well. Dust the top of the torte with cocoa powder and top with the remaining hazelnuts.

ingefärsmaränger

GINGER MERINGUES

makes about 15 large or 30 small meringues

Swedish cuisine definitely imported some old European favorites, and meringues are one of them. This recipe with the addition of ginger is delicious by itself or with whipped cream and strawberries—a good alternative to a strawberry cake. Meringues are often served as part of marängsviss, meringues covered in whipped cream and drizzled in chocolate sauce.

Preheat the oven to 200°F (95°C). Line a baking sheet with a silicone baking mat or parchment paper.

Wipe the inside of a grease-free bowl, preferably stainless steel, with the slice of lemon. Whisk the egg whites in the bowl, ideally with an electric mixer, until white and soft peaks have formed, about 2 minutes. Add the sugar little by little, whisking continuously until the mixture is glossy and stiff peaks form, 5 to 10 minutes. If you turn the bowl upside down, the egg whites should hold. Add the ginger and whisk a bit more.

Lemon slice

3 egg whites, room temperature

¾ cup (5.25 ounces, 148 grams) natural cane sugar

1 teaspoon grated peeled fresh ginger

Using a tablespoon, place the meringue batter in spoonfuls on the baking sheet, about 1 tablespoonful for small meringues and 2 tablespoonfuls for large. You can also pipe out the meringues into shapes using a pastry bag.

Bake for 1½ hours for small meringues or 2 hours for large. When they are done, they should be crisp on the outside and sound hollow. Turn off the oven and leave the meringues in the oven to cool.

Meringues should be stored in an airtight container and will keep for a few weeks.

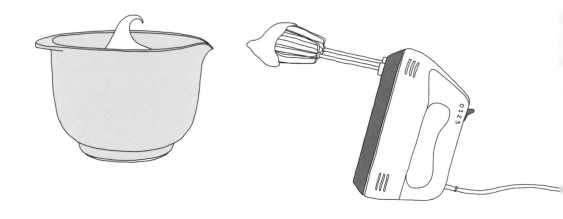

fruktkaka

FRUITCAKE

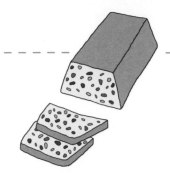

makes one 9-inch (23-centimeter) loaf

Say "fruitcake" to most people and you'll induce a shudder. But this isn't
your stereotypical dry American fruitcake; it's dense, delicious, and
decadent and will be gone within minutes of serving. This recipe comes
from Anna's *mormor* (grandmother) Nellie, who bakes it every year.
Usually made with candied fruit, this cake is even better when you use
real dried fruit, in this case figs and dates. The key, of course, is making
it long before you want to serve it; because it soaks in a whiskey-infused
cheesecloth or gauze wrapping, you want to let it sit for at least a week.

Preheat the oven to 350°F (175°C). Grease and flour a
9 by 5-inch (23 by 12.5-centimeter) loaf pan.

In a large mixing bowl, cream together the butter and
sugar. Mix in 1 egg yolk at a time, stirring until you get
a creamy consistency. Add the figs, dates, currants,
and orange zest to the batter and mix well. Stir in the
flour until well blended.

In a separate bowl, beat the egg whites until stiff
peaks form. Carefully fold into the batter. You will
end up with a thick and chunky batter.

14 tablespoons (7 ounces,
198 grams) unsalted butter,
room temperature

½ cup (3.5 ounces, 99 grams)
natural cane sugar

4 egg yolks

½ cup (2.62 ounces, 75 grams)
dried figs, finely chopped

½ cup (2.62 ounces, 75 grams)
dates, pitted and finely chopped

½ cup (2.5 ounces, 71 grams)
currants

Zest of 1 medium orange

1½ cups (7.5 ounces, 213 grams) all-purpose flour

4 egg whites, room temperature

About ½ cup (120 milliliters) whiskey, cognac, or rum

Using a spatula, scrape the batter into the loaf pan. Bake for 50 to 55 minutes. The fruitcake is done when a toothpick or knife inserted into the center comes out clean. Remove from the oven and let cool. Once cool, remove the fruitcake from the pan.

Place a length of cheesecloth or gauze in a bowl and cover it in the whiskey. Once the fabric has been thoroughly soaked, wrap it around the fruitcake so that the entire cake is covered, then wrap in aluminum foil and store in a cool, dark place for 1 to 4 weeks.

When ready, remove the cake from the wrapping, slice thinly, and serve.

semlor

SWEDISH CREAM BUNS

makes 12 to 16 buns

Semlor are directly linked to the celebration of Fat Tuesday, Fettisdagen, in Sweden. In fact, this sweet bun filled with almond paste and heavy whipped cream is even called a *fettisbulle*, a "fat bun." Rich, sweet, and creamy, it's no surprise that it was historically intended as the kick-off to Lent, but nowadays you find it in cafés and bakeries from New Year's to Easter. If you're working on being traditional, however, make a batch for Fat Tuesday and brew a large batch of French-press coffee to go with it.

In a saucepan, melt the butter; then stir in the milk. Heat until warm to the touch (about 110°F/43°C). In a small bowl, dissolve the yeast in 2 to 3 tablespoons of the warm mixture. Stir and let sit until bubbles form on top of the yeast, about 10 minutes.

In a large bowl, whisk together 1 of the eggs and the sugar. Pour in the remaining butter and milk mixture, along with the yeast, and stir until well blended. Mix in the flour, baking powder, salt, and cardamom. Work the dough together well, by hand or with a wooden spoon.

Transfer the dough to a flat surface and knead it until smooth and elastic, 3 to 5 minutes. The dough should

dough

7 tablespoons (3.5 ounces, 99 grams) unsalted butter

1 cup (240 milliliters) milk

2 teaspoons active dry yeast

2 eggs

¼ cup (1.75 ounces, 50 grams) natural cane sugar

3½ cups (1⅛ pounds, 496 grams) all-purpose flour, or more as needed

1 teaspoon baking powder

½ teaspoon salt

2 teaspoons whole cardamom seeds, crushed

whipped heavy cream

almond paste

powdered sugar

filling

2 cups (10 ounces, 284 grams) blanched almonds

¼ cup (1.75 ounces, 50 grams) natural cane sugar

1 teaspoon pure almond extract

½ to 1 cup (120 to 240 milliliters) milk, depending on dryness of the filling

to finish

½ to 1 cup (120 to 240 milliliters) heavy whipping cream, whipped, for topping, depending on how many semlor you are serving

Confectioners' sugar, for dusting

feel a little wet, but if it sticks to your fingers and the countertop, add a little flour. Go lightly, though; if you add too much, the buns will end up dry. The dough is fully kneaded when you slice into it with a sharp knife and see small air bubbles throughout. Return the dough to the bowl, cover with a clean tea towel, and place in a draft-free place to rise for 45 minutes to an hour.

Grease a baking sheet or line with a silicone baking mat. Divide the dough into 12 to 16 equal parts and roll into balls. Place on the baking sheet with about 2 inches (5 centimeters) between each bun. Cover and let rise for 30 to 45 minutes.

CONTINUED

Preheat the oven to 400°F (200°F).

Whisk the remaining egg and brush on top of the dough balls. Bake for 10 to 15 minutes, until the tops are golden brown. Remove from the oven, transfer the buns to the counter, and cover with a tea towel to let cool.

To prepare the filling, mix the almonds, sugar, and almond extract in a food processor until the almonds are finely ground and the mixture starts to stick together.

Cut a circular "lid" off the top of each bun and set aside. Then cut a circle on the inside of each bun, leaving about ¼ inch (0.5 centimeter) for a border, being careful not to cut all the way through to the bottom. Scoop out the cut portions with a spoon and place in a large bowl. Stir in the almond mixture until well blended. Then pour in enough of the milk to make a filling that's thick and smooth yet not watered down.

Fill the buns with the filling and top with the whipped cream. Place the lid on top of the whipped cream and dust with confectioners' sugar. Serve immediately.

Note: it's rare that anyone makes an entire batch of semlor at one time. The best thing to do is to freeze the leftover buns that aren't going to be eaten that day. When you are ready for another round, defrost them and construct a fresh semla with the appropriate amount of almond filling and whipped cream.

lussekatter

SΛFFRON BUNS

makes 30 to 40 buns

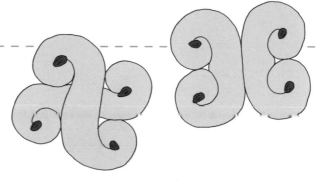

Used in Sweden for centuries, saffron was once the spice of royalty. Nowadays it's still special, but is more readily available and indicative of the Christmas season. Lussekatter are most commonly associated with St. Lucia Day, celebrated on December 13. With religious roots, the modern holiday is a celebration of light; St. Lucia wears a crown of candles on her head. Lussekatter are baked into a variety of shapes, the easiest and most well known being the S shape, but you can get creative with the shapes you make (see pages 114–115).

½ teaspoon saffron threads

Dash of whiskey or cognac

¾ cup (6 ounces, 170 grams) unsalted butter

2 cups (480 milliliters) milk

2 teaspoons active dry yeast

2 eggs

½ cup (3.5 ounces, 99 grams) natural cane sugar

1 teaspoon salt

6½ cups (2 pounds, 923 grams) all-purpose flour, plus more as needed

¾ cup (3.75 ounces, 106 grams) currants (optional), plus more for topping

Using a spoon, crush the saffron in a small bowl. Then add a few drops of whiskey to help fully develop the saffron flavor and set aside.

In a saucepan, melt the butter; then stir in the milk. Heat until warm to the touch (about 110°F/43°C). In a small bowl, dissolve the yeast in 2 to3 tablespoons of the warm mixture. Stir and let sit for a few minutes until bubbles form on top of the yeast.

In a large bowl, whisk 1 of the eggs and blend in the sugar, salt, and saffron mixture. Pour in the remaining butter and milk, along with the yeast, and stir until well blended. Mix in the flour and currants. Work

CONTINUED

together with a wooden spoon or your hands until you can make the dough into a ball.

Transfer the dough to the countertop or other flat surface and knead it until smooth and elastic, 3 to 5 minutes. The dough should feel a little wet, but if it sticks to your fingers and the countertop, add a little flour. Go lightly, though; if you add too much, the buns will end up dry. The dough is fully kneaded when you slice into it with a sharp knife and see small air bubbles throughout. Return the dough to the bowl, cover with a clean tea towel, and place in a draft-free place to rise until doubled in size, about 1 hour.

Grease a baking sheet or line it with parchment paper or a silicone baking mat. Remove the dough from the bowl and roll it into classic saffransbullar shapes (see diagram opposite). Place the buns on the baking sheet with about 1½ inches (4 centimeters) between each bun. Cover and let rise for 30 to 45 minutes. Depending on the size of the buns and baking sheet, you may need to bake in two or three batches. Prepare all the buns at the same time and let them sit, covered with a tea towel, while they wait to bake.

While the dough is rising, preheat the oven to 400°F (200°C).

Whisk the remaining egg and brush on the tops of the buns. Decorate with currants (in the center of where the bun is rolled.)

*julgalt
(Christmas pig)*

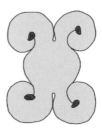

*lussekatt
(Lucia cat)*

Bake for 8 to 10 minutes. Remove from the oven and transfer the buns from the baking sheet to the counter. Cover with a tea towel and let cool before serving.

These buns dry out quickly, so if they are not eaten on the day you bake them, store them in the freezer.

prästens hår
(the hair of the priest)

lindebarnet
(the little baby)

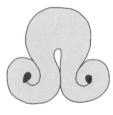

lyran
(the lyre)

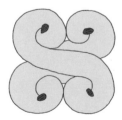

julkuse
(Christmas horse)

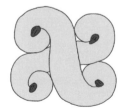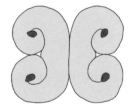

gullvagn
(golden wagon)

saffranskaka med mandelmassa

SAFFRON CAKE WITH ALMOND PASTE

makes one 11-inch (28-centimeter) cake

Swedes do love to put almond paste in a variety of baked goods, and why not in one that's perfect for celebrating the month of December? This recipe, inspired by a cake baked every year by Cecilia, a good family friend of Anna's, is made with half a batch of lussekatter dough, which means you can make half of it into buns and the other half into this sweet and seasonal cake, ideal for serving at an Advent coffee.

Prepare the Lussekatter dough and let rise until doubled in size, about 1 hour.

Mix the almonds, sugar, and almond extract in a food processor until the almonds are almost finely ground and the mixture starts to stick together. If you are using store-bought almonds, you may end up with a coarse, dry meal, which is okay.

In a separate bowl, whisk the egg white, ideally with an electric mixer, until stiff peaks form. Fold into the almond mixture, being careful not to overmix.

Pull off a little less than a fistful of the dough and set aside; you will use this later for decorating the top of the cake. Split the rest of the dough into 2 equal parts and shape them into balls.

½ batch Lussekatter dough (page 113)

1 cup (5 ounces, 142 grams) blanched almonds

¼ cup (1.75 ounces, 50 grams) natural cane sugar

1 teaspoon pure almond extract

1 egg white, room temperature

1 egg, whisked

Currants, for topping

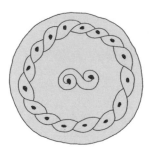

Grease a baking sheet or line it with parchment paper or a silicone baking mat. Transfer the dough to a flat, floured surface. Using a rolling pin, roll out the first ball until it is about 11 inches (28 centimeters) in diameter, or a little less than ¼ inch (0.5 centimeter) thick. Transfer to the baking sheet and spread the almond filling evenly over it. Roll out the second ball in the same manner and place it on top of the filling. Pinch the 2 layers of dough together so that the filling doesn't leak out. Roll out the reserved piece of dough into thin strips and use to decorate the top. Make the classic S shape or a heart, or one of the designs pictured here. Cover the cake with a clean tea towel and let rise for 20 to 30 minutes.

While the dough is rising, preheat the oven to 400°F (200°C).

Brush the top of the cake with the whisked egg and decorate with currants.

Bake for 15 to 20 minutes, until the top is a deep, golden brown. Remove from the oven, carefully transfer to a cooling rack, and cover with a tea towel. When the cake is cool, transfer to a serving platter and slice into wedges.

This cake quickly dries out; if you don't eat the whole thing on the day you bake it, wrap it in aluminum foil to preserve its freshness.

pepparkakor

SWEDISH GINGERSNAPS

makes 40 to 60 cookies, depending on thickness and cookie cutter size

Spicy, crispy, and cut into traditional Swedish shapes like pigs and hearts, nothing says *God Jul*, or "Merry Christmas," like Swedish gingersnaps. There is actually a Swedish expression, *blir snäll av pepparkakor*, which ties back to a myth that, essentially, eating gingersnaps makes you nice. While there are many stories of how this expression came to be, there's no denying that the spices in pepparkakor have many health benefits, which just might give you a positive kick.

There are many recipes for pepparkakor, but this one is just a little spicier than most. Because Swedish sirap is hard to find, we use molasses instead. While Swedes have their traditional pepparkakor shapes, any cookie cutter will work, or you can always use a glass to cut out simple circles. The trick with pepparkakor is that they are supposed to be thin and crispy, so roll them out as thinly as possible. Even if you don't get them super thin, they still bake out well, making them fairly foolproof and an instant holiday classic. The dough must be refrigerated overnight, so plan accordingly.

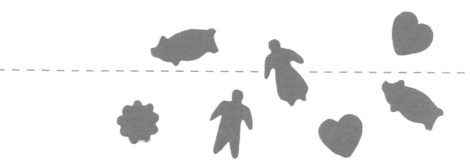

5 tablespoons (2.5 ounces, 71 grams) unsalted butter, room temperature

½ cup (3.5 ounces, 99 grams) natural cane sugar

2 tablespoons molasses

1½ teaspoons ground cloves

1 tablespoon ground cinnamon

1½ teaspoons cardamom seeds, crushed

1 tablespoon ground ginger

¼ teaspoon ground black pepper

½ teaspoon baking soda

1½ cups (7.5 ounces, 213 grams) all-purpose flour

¼ cup (60 milliliters) water

In a large bowl, cream together the butter, sugar, and molasses. Stir in the cloves, cinnamon, cardamom, ginger, pepper, and baking soda and mix until creamy and well blended.

Mix in the flour, a half cup at a time. When you have added about half the flour, blend in the water. Then add the rest of the flour and work together with your hands until a dough forms. It will still be fairly sticky, but you should be able to shape it into a large log. Cover the log in plastic wrap, or wrap it in wax paper, and let sit in the refrigerator overnight.

When ready to bake the cookies, preheat the oven to 375°F (190°C). Grease a baking sheet. You can also use parchment paper or a silicone baking mat, but the cookies get a nicer crispy texture on the underside with a greased sheet.

Cut off a section of the dough from the log, and roll out on a flat, generously floured surface. To avoid sticking to the countertop, roll a little, then flip the

CONTINUED

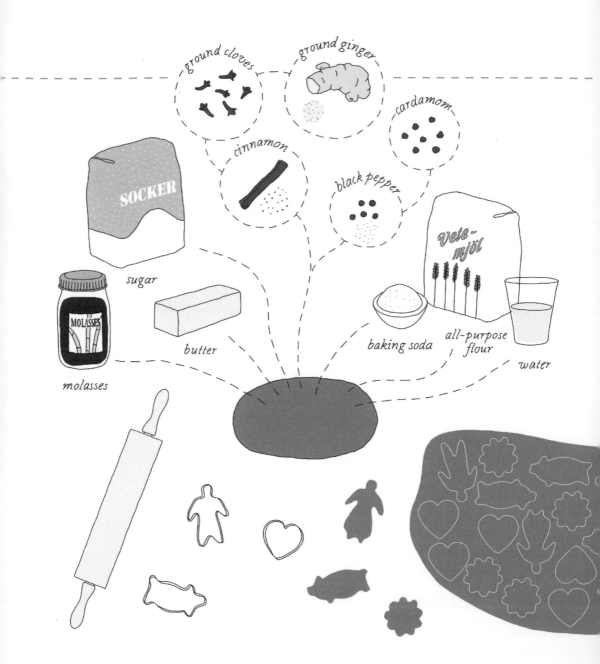

ground cloves

ground ginger

cardamom

cinnamon

black pepper

SOCKER

sugar

Vete-mjöl

MOLASSES

baking soda

all-purpose flour

water

molasses

butter

dough over and roll some more. Add more flour to the surface as needed. Continue in this way until you have rolled the dough as thin as you can get it. The dough is easy to roll out when it's cold, and much stickier as it warms up, so return it to the refrigerator as needed. It's also easiest to roll it out in small batches.

Cut out the dough with cookie cutter forms and place on the baking sheet.

Bake for 5 to 8 minutes, depending on the thickness. These cookies burn easily, so keep an eye on them. Remove from the oven; after 1 or 2 minutes, transfer them from the baking sheet to the counter to cool.

Store in an airtight container.

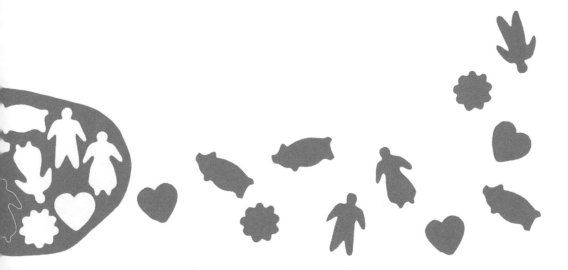

mjuka pepparkakor
SOFT GINGER COOKIES

makes 20 to 25 cookies

These soft gingersnaps are also called *lunchpepparkakor*—that's right, lunch gingersnaps. That's because they're nice and thick, most often spread with a layer of butter and topped with a slice of cheese before being eaten. It's hard to feel hungry after that combination and a cup of coffee or mug of tea. Other good ways to eat these are with a thin layer of marmalade or some blue cheese spread on top. They're good on their own too, of course. The dough must be refrigerated at least overnight, so plan accordingly.

In a saucepan, mix the molasses and sugar together over medium heat until you get a smooth but runny consistency. Stir in the butter, cloves, ginger, cinnamon, cardamom, and pepper until the butter has completely melted. Remove from the heat and set aside to cool for 15 minutes.

In a large bowl, whisk together the egg and milk. Pour in the molasses mixture and stir together.

In a separate bowl, combine the flour, baking powder, baking soda, and salt. Add to the egg and molasses mixture and work everything together until you get a smooth and even batter. The batter will be very sticky. Cover the bowl and let sit in the refrigerator for 24 to 48 hours.

¾ cup (180 milliliters) molasses

½ cup (3.75 ounces, 106 grams) firmly packed brown sugar

¼ cup (2 ounces, 57 grams) unsalted butter

2 teaspoons ground cloves

2 to 3 teaspoons ground ginger

2 teaspoons ground cinnamon

2 teaspoons whole cardamom seeds, crushed

¼ teaspoon ground black pepper

1 egg

¼ cup (60 milliliters) milk

2½ cups (12.5 ounces, 355 grams) all-purpose flour

1 teaspoon baking powder
1 teaspoon baking soda
¼ teaspoon salt

When ready to bake the cookies, preheat the oven to 400°F (200°C). Grease a baking sheet or line it with parchment paper or a silicone baking mat

Pull off golf-ball-size pieces of dough and roll into balls. Place on the baking sheet and flatten out to about ½ inch (1.25 centimeters) thick. The flattened cookies should not be less than 1 inch (2.5 centimeters) apart on the baking sheet. The dough is easy to roll out when it's cold, and much stickier as it warms up, so if you need to, put it back in the refrigerator to chill. It can also be helpful to wet your hands before rolling, as it keeps the dough from sticking too much.

Bake for 12 to 15 minutes, depending on the size of the cookies. Remove from the oven, then transfer the cookies to the counter to cool.

Once completely cooled, store in an airtight container.

mandelmusslor

ALMOND TARTLET SHELLS

makes about 25 tartlets, depending on the size of the tins

Thin and buttery, these almond tartlet shells are perfect for a Christmas dessert. Typically, they are filled with a berry jam and heavy whipped cream. Serve them with a glass of port before opening your presents on Christmas Eve, in true Swedish fashion. Classic mandelmusslor tins, which come in triangles, diamonds, and circles, are hard to come by outside Scandinavia, unless you manage to score a set at a vintage store or estate sale, but small tartlet tins work. Mandelmusslor have a reputation for being a little difficult to make, and it's common to lose a few in the baking process as they sometimes break when removing them from the tins. So butter the tins liberally; if some do crumble and break, see it as an opportunity to get a little delicious payment for your hard work. Serve plain or filled with jam or berries and topped with heavy whipped cream.

In a food processor, grind the almonds until finely ground.

Cream together the butter and sugar. Add the almonds, almond extract, and egg to the mixture and work together until well blended. Work in all of the flour in small increments until the dough sticks together. Cover and let the dough sit in the refrigerator for 30 minutes to an hour.

1 cup (5 ounces, 142 grams) blanched almonds

7 tablespoons (3.5 ounces, 99 grams) unsalted butter, room temperature

¼ cup (1.75 ounces, 50 grams) natural cane sugar

½ teaspoon pure almond extract

1 small egg

1 cup (5 ounces, 142 grams) all-purpose flour

When you are ready to bake the tartlets, preheat the oven to 400°F (200°C). Generously grease small tart tins with butter.

Depending on the size of your tins, pinch off a walnut-size piece of dough and press it into the tin. Make sure that the dough is pressed all the way up the sides of the tin and is evenly distributed and pressed very thinly. If the dough gets too sticky, put it back in the refrigerator to chill for a while.

Bake for 8 to 10 minutes, until the edges of the tartlets are a light golden brown. Remove from the oven; when the tins are cool enough to touch, carefully tap the tartlet shells out. Let cool on the counter.

glögg
SWEDISH MULLED WINE

makes 4 to 6 servings

In the bitter cold of winter, serving a warm drink is one of the nicest gestures a host or hostess can make, and while coffee is important for a Swedish Advent celebration, glögg is even more so. Swedish mulled wine is commonly served throughout the month of December, at Christmas work parties and afternoon gatherings and on Christmas Day itself. Given the cold of Swedish winter, it's no surprise that Swedes want to warm up with a spicy mulled wine, and even if you're not in a white winter wonderland, it still tastes good.

When you serve the glögg, put it out alongside a tray of Swedish Gingersnaps (page 118), which go perfectly with the steaming hot drink. A nonalcoholic version of glögg can also be made with a base of black currant cordial.

Cut the figs into halves or quarters. Soak them, together with the raisins, orange zest, ginger, cinnamon, cloves, and cardamom, in the rum for at least 4 hours or overnight.

After letting the rum sit, strain to remove the fruit and spices. Set the figs aside to be used later.

5 dried figs

30 raisins, plus more for garnish

1 tablespoon orange zest

1 to 2 tablespoons chopped peeled fresh ginger

3 cinnamon sticks

2 teaspoons whole cloves

5 whole green cardamom pods

¾ cup (180 milliliters) rum, whiskey, or cognac

1 bottle (750 milliliters) full-bodied red wine (such as Cabernet Sauvignon or Syrah)

½ cup (3.75 ounces, 106 grams) firmly packed brown sugar

Blanched almonds, for garnish

In a saucepan, heat the wine, and add in the sugar and the spiced rum. Stir until the sugar has dissolved completely, making sure not to let it boil.

To serve, pour into small mugs with a few blanched almonds, raisins, and figs in each.

CHAPTER 5

- - - - - -

bread, sandwiches, and fika as a snack

there is a common perception among non-Swedes about Stieg Larsson's *Millennium* series: "All they do is sit around and drink coffee and eat open-face sandwiches!" To Swedes, the obsession with coffee and open-face sandwiches does not seem odd, or even noticeable for that matter. In Sweden a cup of coffee and an open-face sandwich, known in Swedish as a *smörgås* or in the more familiar usage, *macka*, are as common as a cup of tea before bed or drinking water to rehydrate after a workout. That's the beautiful thing about fika: not only can it be a coffee break, but in a pinch, it can also serve as a quick meal.

The Swedes have a wonderful expression called *mellanmål*; literally translated, it means "the in-between meal." While in the United States we refer to such things as snack food, a mellanmål is a healthier step above, often consisting of fruit or a hearty sandwich; it is intended to be filling and good for you. For children after school, this often consists of a smörgås and a glass of milk or saft, the Swedish fruit cordial.

swedish breads

There are many types of breads and rolls that fall into the mellanmål category, some perfect for a lunch sandwich and others the little pick-me-up that you often need in the slow hours of the afternoon. Maybe the most well known of Swedish breads outside Scandinavian geographical boundaries is crispbread. Said to have originated somewhere around AD 500, *knäckebröd*, as it is called in Swedish, is a culinary staple. It comes in a variety of forms, from big circles that are snapped into pieces to precise rectangles. Perfecting the art of baking it can take time, and bakers can spend their entire careers mastering their unique version of knäckebröd.

But knäckebröd is only one of the types of bread that a smörgås can be made with. There is *Tunnbröd*, the Swedish Flatbread (page 134), which is rolled up and perfect for taking along as a travel snack; *skorpor*, crisp rolls that are twice baked until they are extra light and dry; and the hearty loaves of dense bread, like rye bread, spiced with tastes like caraway, fennel, and anise that Scandinavian cuisine is known for. It all goes well with extra strong coffee or a big cup of tea, of course.

Making the perfect smörgås is also an art, an experience in pairing flavors and not being afraid to stack a piece of bread high with whatever strikes your imagination. The piece of bread, no matter what kind, is simply a building block for constructing the rest.

But it's not just the smörgås that can serve as a meal. Swedes also have the Swedish Pancakes (page 138). Much like in France, the thin version of the pancake is served at lunch or even dinner, as a second course after soup. The thin, crepe-like pancake comes from a time when there was no such thing as an oven; all people had was an iron pan that could be placed over a fire. A commonplace dish in the Swedish kitchen, the pancake's close relation is *plättar*, which can be made using the same batter as regular Swedish pancakes, but fried in a special pan that makes seven small pancake rounds.

So whether it's a sandwich, a pancake, or a round of savory Swedish scones, you might just find yourself once in a while replacing a meal with fika instead.

how to make a smörgås

While you can stick to traditional pairings when building your smörgås, there are no smörgås police out there; you are limited only by your creativity. Pair a layer of cheese with sliced cucumber, bell pepper, or even apple. Add a leaf of lettuce to rye bread slathered with butter and top it off with a slice of salami. Just be sure you start with a good base, be it rye bread, crisp rolls, or even something as simple as a crispbread cracker (page 152). Here are some of the classics.

- A meatball **MACKA**, made with halved meatballs on a creamy beet salad, preferably on rye bread.

- A **SKORPA** with a layer of butter, a medium-hard cheese like Swiss or Jarlsberg, and marmalade.

- **TUNNBRÖD** spread with *leverpastej*, a spreadable liver pâté, topped with sweet and crisp pickled cucumber, and rolled into a wrap.

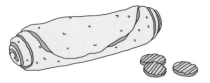

- **RÄKMACKA**, a shrimp sandwich made by layering lettuce, sliced eggs, mayonnaise, shrimp, and dill on toasted bread.

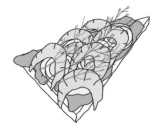

- **SILLMACKA**, made by placing pickled herring, sour cream, red onion, and chives on dark rye bread.

- **GRAVLAX**, made on dark or light bread, toasted or plain, topped with Swedish cured salmon, mustard sauce, and dill (we also like it on knäckebröd).

recipes

Here is a selection of recipes to give you the perfect base of breads for mellanmål, from savory scones to simple crispbread crackers, so that you can enjoy smörgås at home.

tunnbröd

SWEDISH FLATBREAD

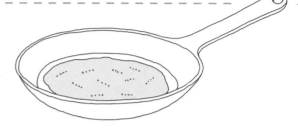

makes 18 to 20 flatbread rounds

Tunnbröd is sort of like the Swedish tortilla; the flatbread can be used to wrap just about anything. Light and easy to roll, it's a popular bread for making sandwiches to travel with—just choose your filling and roll up in some aluminum foil. In Sweden, a common picnic food is made by spreading the tunnbröd with leverpastej (spreadable liver pâté) and topping it off with sweet and crisp pickled cucumber slices. Traditionally, tunnbröd are rolled out with a kruskavel (see page 12), a knobby rolling pin that gives tunnbröd its classic texture. These tunnbröd rounds are baked in a dry frying pan, a fun baking process that leaves you with a batch of delicious flatbread ready to be eaten right away or packed up for fika on the go.

In a saucepan, melt the butter; then stir in the milk. Heat until warm to the touch (about 110°F/43°C). In a small bowl, dissolve the yeast in a few tablespoons of the warm mixture. Stir and let sit for a few minutes until bubbles form on top of the yeast.

In a large bowl, mix together the flours, sugar, anise seeds, and salt. Stir in the remaining butter and milk followed by the yeast mixture. Work the dough together with your hands and knead it on a flat, floured surface until smooth and elastic. Return the

3 tablespoons (1.5 ounces, 43 grams) unsalted butter

1½ cups (360 milliliters) milk

2 teaspoons active dry yeast

3 cups (15 ounces, 426 grams) all-purpose flour

¾ cup (3.25 ounces, 90 grams) rye flour

1 tablespoon brown sugar

1 tablespoon anise seeds, crushed

½ teaspoon salt

dough to the bowl, cover with a clean tea towel, and let rise in a warm, draft-free place for about an hour.

Divide the dough into 18 to 20 pieces (depending on the size of your frying pan). On a floured surface, roll each of the balls out to a flat round, about ⅛ inch (0.5 centimeter) thick. As you roll them out, stack them with some sprinkled flour in between each round.

Before baking, roll each round with a kruskavel or make a pattern by poking the dough with a fork. The pattern helps the bread stay flat when baking. If you want to skip this step entirely, just puncture the air bubbles that appear while baking the bread, so that the bread stays nice and flat.

Bake each round in a hot, dry frying pan (use a cast-iron or other thick-bottom pan) for about 1 minute per side. If you feel up to it, have 2 frying pans going at the same time to speed up the process. Note that using your cast-iron pan in this way will dry it out, so make sure to properly oil it when you are finished.

Stack flatbreads in a tea towel and cover them so that they retain their heat. Serve warm. Leftover flatbread should be frozen in an airtight container.

If you don't want to bake the entire batch at the same time, you can store the dough, covered with plastic wrap, in the refrigerator and roll it out the next day.

svenska scones

SWEDISH SCONES

makes 2 large scone rounds, enough for 4 people

While you might be thinking of typical British scones, the Swedish version is a bit more like soda bread. Because it's easy to bake and comes together in very little time, it's a wonderful recipe when you want the taste of home-baked goods to go with your morning coffee but don't want to stand in the kitchen too long. Caraway is often used in Swedish breads and rolls, and in this version, paired with sunflower seeds, it gives just enough of a savory bite. Serve with butter and Fig Preserves (page 146) or Queen's Jam (page 91). To make like a true Swede, pair the jam with a slice of cheese.

Preheat the oven to 480°F (250°C). Grease a baking sheet or line it with parchment paper or a silicone baking mat.

Toast the caraway seeds and the sunflower seeds together in a frying pan over medium heat. When the seeds start to color and have a nice aroma, turn off the heat and remove them immediately from the pan. Place the seeds in a bowl and let them cool for a few minutes.

Sift the flour together with the baking powder and salt. Add the butter in small pieces and work together with your fingertips until the dough resembles a

1 teaspoon whole caraway seeds

3 tablespoons raw sunflower seeds

2¾ cups (13.75 ounces, 390 grams) all-purpose flour

1½ teaspoons baking powder

1 teaspoon salt

5 tablespoons (2.5 ounces, 71 grams) unsalted butter

1 cup (240 milliliters) milk

coarse meal. Mix in the seeds; then stir in the milk and mix together quickly to get a semisticky dough. Don't knead the dough.

Divide the dough into 2 equal parts and shape them into 6-inch (15-centimeter) rounds. Place the two rounds 2 inches apart on the baking sheet and, using a knife, score into quarters, cutting only part way through the dough. Poke a pattern into the top of the scones with a fork. Bake for 20 to 25 minutes, until the scones are a light golden brown. Remove from the oven and let cool slightly before breaking along the scored lines into quarters. Serve warm.

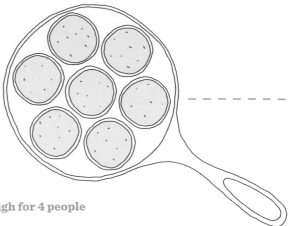

pannkakor

SWEDISH PANCAKES

makes 16 to 20 pancakes, enough for 4 people

Much like crepes, Swedish pancakes are thin and delicate. They fry up easily in any frying pan, which makes them a common lunch item at home and at schools. They are typically served spread with jam and sprinkled with granulated sugar, then rolled up. Unless you're very hungry, you might be hard pressed to eat more than 4 pancakes, but that's a good thing: leftovers can be taken along as a snack on an outing. For a more decadent treat, serve them with heavy whipped cream.

In a small saucepan, melt the butter. Remove from the heat and set aside to cool.

In a bowl, whisk together the eggs and half of the milk. Stir in the flour and salt and mix well. Pour in the rest of the milk and the slightly cooled butter and mix until you get a smooth, liquid batter.

You want to fry these pancakes fairly hot, so heat a cast-iron frying pan or nonstick skillet over medium-high heat. Put in a teaspoon or two of butter. When the butter has melted, pour in ⅛ to ⅓ cup (30 to 80 milliliters) of batter, depending on how large you want your pancakes and the size of your frying pan. Keep in mind that Swedish pancakes are meant to be very thin, almost like crepes, so make sure the batter

pancakes

3 tablespoons (1.5 ounces, 43 grams) unsalted butter, plus more for frying

3 eggs

2½ cups (600 milliliters) milk

1 cup (5 ounces, 142 grams) all-purpose flour

½ teaspoon salt

topping

Jam

spreads out evenly in the pan. You can also tilt the pan a bit in order to cover the whole surface with batter. Cook until the pancake has set and the sides begin to pull away from the pan, just a couple of minutes per side. To double-check that they are ready to flip, pull up a side of the pancake; it should be a very light golden brown.

Serve immediately with jam or a sprinkle of granulated sugar.

Store extras in an airtight container in the refrigerator.

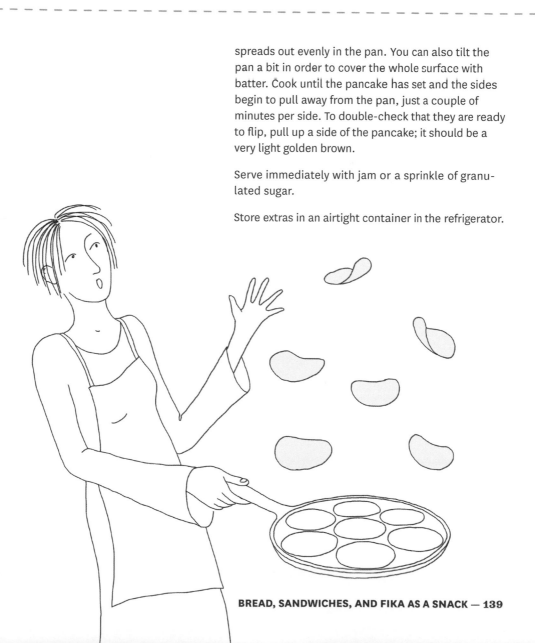

kumminskorpor

CARAWAY CRISPS

makes about 40 crisps

Skorpor are a favorite in the Swedish repertoire of breads and rolls. They are basically slices (like in this recipe) or rolls that are cut in half and toasted until they dry out, making them easy to store for extended periods of time. Here we have baked them in loaves and then sliced them. The twice-baked skorpor are crispy and airy, and most commonly slathered in a healthy layer of butter. While they can be either sweet or savory, this recipe adds a little caraway to give the skorpor a truly Swedish taste.

In a saucepan, melt the butter; then stir in the milk. Heat until warm to the touch (about 110°F/43°C). In a small bowl, dissolve the yeast in 2 to 3 tablespoons of the warm mixture. Stir and let sit for a few minutes until bubbles form on top of the yeast.

In a large bowl, mix together the flour, sugar, caraway seeds, baking powder, and salt. Stir in the remaining butter and milk, followed by the yeast mixture. Work the dough together well with your hands.

Transfer the dough to a flat surface and knead it until smooth and elastic, 3 to 5 minutes. The dough should feel moist, but if it sticks to your fingers or the countertop, add a little flour. The dough is fully kneaded when you slice into it with a sharp knife and

5 tablespoons (2.5 ounces, 71 grams) unsalted butter

1 cup (240 milliliters) milk

2 teaspoons active dry yeast

3 cups (15 ounces, 426 grams) all-purpose flour, or more as needed

¼ cup (1.75 ounces, 50 grams) natural cane sugar

2 teaspoons caraway seeds, crushed

1 teaspoon baking powder

¼ teaspoon salt

see small air bubbles throughout. Return the dough to the bowl, cover with a clean tea towel, and place in a draft-free place to rise for about an hour.

Grease a baking sheet or line it with parchment paper or a silicone baking mat. Divide the dough into 2 equal pieces and carefully shape each piece into a 12-inch- (30.5-centimeter-) long loaf, about 1½ inches (4 centimeters) thick. Place on the baking sheet, cover, and let rise for about 45 minutes.

While the bread is rising, preheat the oven to 450°F (230°C).

When the loaves have finished rising, bake for 10 to 15 minutes, until they are golden brown. Remove from the oven and let cool. Maintain oven temperature.

Using a knife, cut both loaves into 20 equally sized slices. Place the slices close together on the baking sheet and toast at 450°F (230°C) until they have a nice golden color, about 5 minutes. If the baking sheet doesn't fit all the slices, divide them onto two baking sheets. Both sheets can be baked at the same time, but be sure to switch them from upper to lower levels in the oven halfway through. Lower the heat to 200°F (95°C) to dry out the rolls for 20 to 30 minutes. Turn the oven off and leave the rolls in the oven for 4 to 5 hours more until they are dry, light, and crispy.

If you bake these in the evening, you can also leave them in overnight and take them out in the morning. Store in an airtight container.

rostade rågbullar

TOASTED RYE BUNS

makes 24 to 32 bun halves

Traditional skorpor are baked until they dry out, but in this version, you get a roll that remains a little doughy on the inside with a crispy top, perfect for pairing with a little jam and a morning cup of coffee. This recipe comes from Anna's mormor (grandmother) Nellie, who always has these on hand in the freezer; they're easy to defrost, spread with butter, add a bit of cheese, and top with apple slices. The recipe has just enough rye flour in it to give it a heartier taste that makes it as good for breakfast as for fika.

In a saucepan, melt the butter; then stir in the milk. Heat until warm to the touch (about 110°F/43°C). In a small bowl, dissolve the yeast in 2 to 3 tablespoons of the warm mixture. Stir and let sit for a few minutes until bubbles form on top of the yeast.

Once the yeast has dissolved, add it to the remaining butter and milk mixture in a large bowl. Stir in the flours, sugar, and salt and mix well. Work together with a wooden spoon or your hands until you can make the dough into a ball. Return the dough to the bowl, cover with a clean tea towel, and let rise for an hour.

Grease a baking sheet or line it with parchment paper or a silicone baking mat. Transfer the dough to a flat, floured surface and knead it until smooth and elastic;

2 tablespoons (1 ounce, 28 grams) unsalted butter

2 cups (480 milliliters) milk

2 teaspoons active dry yeast

4 cups (1¼ pounds, 568 grams) all-purpose flour

1 cup (4.25 ounces, 120 grams) rye flour

¼ cup (1.75 ounces, 50 grams) natural cane sugar

1 teaspoon salt

1 egg, beaten

if you poke the dough, it should spring back. Separate into 12 to 16 equally sized pieces and roll into round balls. Place the balls on the baking sheet, cover, and let rise for 45 minutes.

While the buns are rising, preheat the oven to 450°F (230°C).

When the buns have finished rising, brush the tops with the beaten egg.

Bake for 8 to 10 minutes, until the buns are golden brown. Remove the buns from the oven and turn up the oven to 480°F (250°C).

When the buns are cool enough to touch, cut them in half, horizontally. This works best with a serrated knife. Place the halves back on the baking sheet, with the cut side up. Put back in the oven to toast until golden brown, 5 to 7 minutes.

Serve immediately, or let cool on a cooling rack and store in the freezer.

anis och hasselnöts biscotti

ANISE AND HAZELNUT BISCOTTI

makes 36 cookies

Biscotti is obviously not a traditional Swedish recipe, but with their love of crisp rolls, it's no surprise that Swedes would crave a sweet, crispy cookie to go with their coffee as well. Biscotti are the perfect match, and in this recipe, typical Nordic anise flavor is paired with hazelnuts for a tasty cookie that's meant to be dipped in your coffee.

Preheat the oven to 350°F (175°C). Grease a baking sheet or line it with parchment paper or a silicone baking mat.

Toast the hazelnuts in a skillet over medium heat until they start to pop and have some color. Let cool; then coarsely chop.

Cream the butter and sugar until well blended. Add the eggs one by one and whisk to a smooth and even batter.

In a separate bowl, mix together the flour, baking powder, salt, anise, and hazelnuts. Fold the mixture into the butter and eggs and mix until well blended. The batter will be sticky.

1 cup (5 ounces, 142 grams) raw hazelnuts

¼ cup (2 ounces, 57 grams) unsalted butter, room temperature

1 cup (7.5 ounces, 213 grams) firmly packed brown sugar

2 eggs

1⅔ cups (8.33 ounces, 236 grams) all-purpose flour

1 teaspoon baking powder

¼ teaspoon salt

4 teaspoons whole anise seeds, coarsely crushed

Shape the dough into 2 logs about 12 inches (30.5 centimeters) long and 1½ inches (4 centimeters) thick and place them on the baking sheet.

Bake for 15 to 20 minutes, until the logs are baked all the way through and the tops are golden brown. Remove from the oven and lower the heat to 300°F (150°C).

Let the logs cool for 10 minutes, then carefully transfer to a cutting board. Using a serrated knife, cut the cookies diagonally into 18 equally sized pieces.

Lay each piece flat on the baking sheet and bake for 15 minutes. Remove from the oven, turn each piece over, and bake for an additional 15 minutes. If the cookies still feel a little soft, bake them a few more minutes. Remove from the oven and let cool completely. Store in an airtight container.

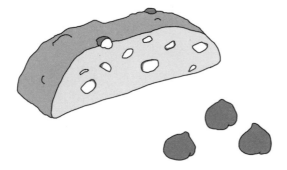

fikonmarmelad

FIG PRESERVES

makes about 1¹/₃ cups (320 milliliters)

While fresh figs aren't common in Sweden, dried figs are often used in Swedish baking. Using dried figs, you can easily make your own jam. While most jams are made by boiling fruit with sugar, the combination of figs and port makes this jam sweet enough on its own, and gives it a distinct flavor. It's an ideal jam to use in Jam Thumbprint Cookies (page 40) or Almond Tartlet Shells (page 124) and is the central ingredient in Fig Squares (page 38). It also works as a spread for Crispbread Crackers (page 152) or Toasted Rye Buns (page 142).

Cut the figs into smaller pieces and place them in a bowl. Pour over the port so that it covers the figs, and let sit for 1 to 2 hours. After soaking, the figs should become a little softer.

About 1½ cups (about 8 ounces, 227 grams) chopped dried figs

1 cup (240 milliliters) port wine, or more as needed

Pour the figs and port into a saucepan and bring the mixture to a boil. Lower the heat and slowly cook for about 10 minutes. By this point, the figs should have started to fall apart and the port will have reduced. If the figs get too dry, add a little more port or a splash of water and let simmer a bit longer.

Remove from the heat and let cool. Once it's cool enough to handle, place the mixture in a food processor. Pulse until you have preserves that are thick, smooth, and spreadable.

Store the preserves in a clean glass jar in the refrigerator for up to a week. If you are not planning to eat the jam right away, you can also store it in the freezer.

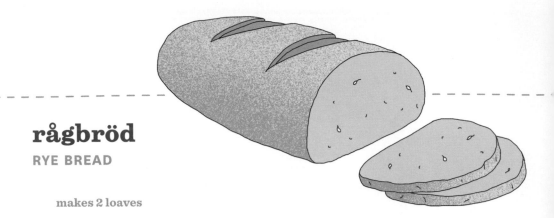

rågbröd

RYE BREAD

makes 2 loaves

Freshly baked bread is a tradition in Sweden, as evidenced by the number of bakeries you will find in any Swedish city. But home baked is always best, and this hearty rye bread is the perfect base for any kind of smörgås. This recipe uses an old Swedish tradition of scalding the rye flour before making the bread. This makes for a richer and fuller bread. Adapted from the book *Vår Kokbok*, this recipe uses prunes, which gives it just the right sweet flavor, in place of the traditional Swedish mörk sirap (dark syrup).

To prepare the first dough, place the flour in a bowl. Bring the water to a boil and pour it over the flour. Work the flour and the water together with a large spoon or spatula. The dough will be very sticky. Cover the bowl and let stand at room temperature until completely cool. For best results, the dough should sit for 6 to 8 hours or overnight.

first dough

3 cups (12.75 ounces, 362 grams) rye flour

3 cups (720 milliliters) water

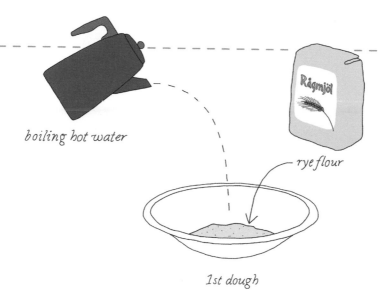

boiling hot water

rye flour

1st dough

second dough

4 teaspoons active dry yeast

5 tablespoons warm water (about 110°F/43°C)

8 prunes

4 teaspoons whole anise seeds

3 cups (15 ounces, 426 grams) all-purpose flour, plus more as needed

2 teaspoons salt

To prepare the second dough, in a small bowl, dissolve the yeast in 2 tablespoons of the warm water. Let sit for about 10 minutes.

In a blender or food processor, mix together the prunes and the remaining 3 tablespoons of water until you get a smooth and sticky consistency.

Crush the anise seeds slightly with a mortar and pestle. In a large bowl, mix them with the flour and salt. Add the yeast, the prunes, and the first dough. Work together well. This dough is heavy and a little hard to work with; instead of working together in the bowl, you may prefer to work it directly on the countertop.

CONTINUED

Transfer the dough to a flat surface and knead it with as little extra flour as possible. The dough should be a little sticky and dense. In fact, it may feel so dense that you will fear it baking into a hard rock. Not to worry, it won't. Return the dough to the bowl, cover, and let rise for 45 minutes.

Grease a baking sheet. Divide the dough into 2 equal pieces and shape each piece into a 12-inch- (30.5-centimeter-) long loaf. Place on the baking sheet, cover, and let rise for about an hour. The loaves will have small cracks on the surface.

While the bread is rising, preheat the oven to 400°F (200°C).

When the loaves have finished rising, bake for about 40 minutes. The bread should become a dark brown color; if you knock at the bottom of the loaf, it should have a hollow sound. Remove from the oven and let the loaves cool completely on a cooling rack before slicing.

The bread will keep 2 to 3 days in a paper or plastic bag. To store longer, freeze the bread once it has cooled, either whole or sliced.

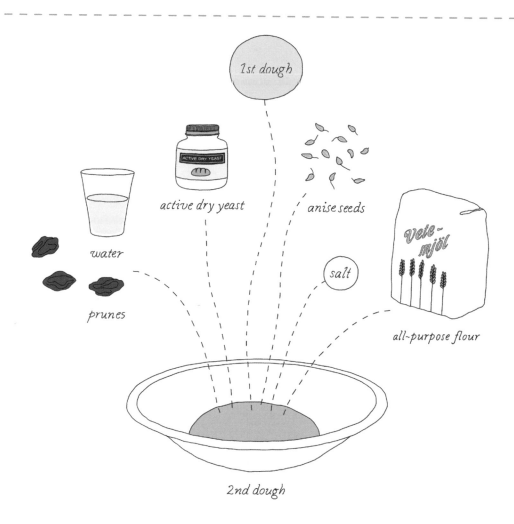

1st dough

active dry yeast

anise seeds

water

Vete-mjöl

salt

prunes

all-purpose flour

2nd dough

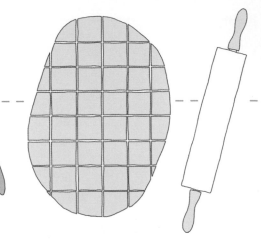

knäckekex
CRISPBREAD CRACKERS

makes 100 to 120 crackers

Knäckebröd is right up there with meatballs and herring in terms of iconic Swedish food. The crispbread that is served with almost every meal is a staple in most Swedish households. Baking traditional knäckebröd is an involved process, and it's so readily available in Sweden that few people venture to make it themselves. This cracker version, however, is a simpler way to try your hand at making this culinary cornerstone. If you don't have caraway seeds on hand, rosemary, crushed fennel, or anise seeds are also excellent toppings. These crackers are delicious served with a little chèvre and Fig Preserves (page 148) or as a typical Swedish smörgås with sliced cucumber.

Heat the water until warm to the touch but not scalding, about 110°F (43°C). In a small bowl, dissolve the yeast in 2 to 3 tablespoons of the water. Stir a few times and mix in the honey. Let the mixture sit for about 10 minutes, until bubbles form on top of the yeast.

In a large bowl, mix together the flours, the yeast mixture, and the remaining water. Work together well with your hands, until you can make the dough into a ball.

Transfer the dough to a lightly floured flat surface and knead it for about 2 minutes. The dough should feel slightly sticky. Return the dough to the bowl, cover,

1 cup (240 milliliters) water

1 teaspoon active dry yeast

2 teaspoons honey

1 cup (4.25 ounces, 120 grams) rye flour

1¾ cups (8.75 ounces, 248 grams) all-purpose flour, plus more as needed

1 tablespoon caraway seeds, toasted (see page 136) and crushed

2 teaspoons flaky sea salt

and let rise at room temperature in a draft-free place for at least 6 hours or overnight. The dough can also rise overnight in the refrigerator; remove it from the refrigerator an hour before you plan to bake.

When ready to bake, preheat the oven to 400°F (200°C). Grease a baking sheet with olive oil. Add the caraway seeds and sea salt to the dough and knead it for about 2 minutes on a lightly floured flat surface. Add more flour if necessary. The dough should feel smooth and the surface should not feel sticky.

Divide the dough into 8 equal balls. Flour a flat surface and your rolling pin and roll out each ball until very thin (as thin as the caraway seeds). To prevent the dough from sticking, it's a good idea to roll a little, add flour to the surface if needed, then flip the dough over and roll some more. Continue until the dough is rolled thin.

Cut the dough into 3-inch (8-centimeter) squares using a pastry cutter or a sharp knife; then lightly roll them one more time. Place as many as you can fit on the baking sheet.

Bake for 5 to 8 minutes, until the crackers are golden brown and crispy. If they are still soft, bake them just a little longer. They burn easily, so keep an eye them. Remove from the oven and let sit for a few minutes before placing them on a cooling rack.

When completely cool, store in an airtight container.

resources

There are several key Swedish baking ingredients that can't be found in your average grocery store. Here are a few online resources for tracking down specialty items.

SCANDINAVIAN SPECIALTIES www.scanspecialties.com

MARINA MARKET www.marinamarket.com

SCANDINAVIAN BUTIK www.scandinavianbutik.com

WIKSTRÖM'S SPECIALTY FOODS www.wikstromsgourmet.com

acknowledgments

A book always has an author, or in this case two, but while one or two names may grace the cover, there is inevitably a long list of people that made that book possible. Fika would not have come to be had it not been for family, friends, and sometimes even strangers who were willing to take a few extra cookies off our hands.

Neither of us would have started baking had it not been for our mothers. And neither of them would have baked the Swedish classics without the memories of their own mothers. Therefore, this book wouldn't have come to life had it not been for mormor Gertrud, mormor Nellie, mamma Mona, and mamma Britta. Thanks to all of you for both inspiration, encouragement, and many of the recipes that make this book what it is. We are truly grateful.

Thank you as well to Helka, the Åström family, aunt Lotta, Cecilia Blomberg, and Göran the gardener for their recipes, as well as morfar Markus for teaching Anna at an early age the incredible importance of always having a treat with coffee, and glögg for breakfast on Christmas Eve.

To pappa Lennart who made sure that Johanna always had good drawing supplies growing up, and to pappa Norman who meticulously designed a gingerbread house pattern every Christmas to bake and assemble with Anna.

To Marek Walczak and Luc Revel who made sure that we both stayed fully caffeinated through the writing, drawing, and baking process.

Thank you to Amy DuFault for being the first one to think that the two of us should connect. She was right.

To all of the people that were willing to test recipes and take on a fika overflow in their kitchens: Renee Baumann, Emily Dilling, Jessie Kanelos Weiner, Kristen Beddard Heimann, and mamma Britta. And yes, even to pappa

Norman who isn't known to bake much, but was happy to test his very favorite recipe, Märtas.

To everyone that provided all kinds of baking advice, particularly Renee Baumann, Ibán Yarza and Andrew Janjigian.

To Kurt Andersson for making the best kaffegök; Gunni Nilsson for always having cookies at home when young Johanna came to visit; Sara Högberg for tunnbröd inspiration; and to Johanna's twin sister, Anna Kindvall, for being such a wonderful childhood baking partner.

To Rachel Meyer, Megan Ponder, and Xochil Springer for being there with bubbles, both in person and in spirit; and to Dave Hoffman for his solid policy of always leaving containers filled with cookies on people's doorsteps. And to Anna's "extra" aunts Cecilia and Ann-Marie who along with her mother ensured she grew up with a good dose of Swedish culture despite being geographically far away.

To every single person that enjoyed a bit of fika when our own freezers and cookie tins were completely full: Frank Gurdak, Vivian Selbo, Carl Skelton, Pearl, Veronika Kindvall, Oskar Kindvall, Olle Kindvall, Robert Ek, Susie Rasmussen, Oda, Marek, Luc, Britta, Norman, Emily, Kristen, and Jessie.

To our lovely book designer, Betsy Stromberg—your hard work and great taste have made our book look so great. You brought fika to life!

And finally to our wonderful editor, Kaitlin Ketchum, who somehow came across our book proposal and believed in it enough to make this all come together, thank you from the bottom of our hearts for helping us embark on this adventure. We owe you a fika or two.

index

Published in the United States by Ten Speed Press,
an imprint of the Crown Publishing Group, a division of
Random House LLC, a Penguin Random House Company,
New York.
www.crownpublishing.com
www.tenspeed.com

Ten Speed Press and the Ten Speed Press colophon are
registered trademarks of Random House LLC.

Library of Congress Cataloging-in-Publication Data

Brones, Anna, author.
Fika : the art of the Swedish coffee break, with recipes
for pastries, breads, and other treats / Anna Brones.
    pages cm
Includes bibliographical references and index.
1. Cooking, Swedish. 2. Snack foods—Sweden.
3. Rest periods—Sweden. I. Title.
TX722.S8B76 2015
641.59485—dc23
                          2014034412

Hardcover ISBN: 978-1-60774-586-0
eBook ISBN: 978-1-60774-587-7

Printed in China

Design by Betsy Stromberg

Recipes adapted and developed by Anna Brones and
Johanna Kindvall